CONTESTING
DEMOCRATIC
DEFICIT

PRAISE FOR THE BOOK

Rarely does a book achieve what this book does—marrying an insider's perspective with objectivity. This is political insight and analysis at its finest. Essential reading for anyone seeking to understand the power dynamics, ideological clashes and historic voter mandates in one of the most consequential elections in Indian history.

Manoj Kumar Jha, Member of Parliament (Rajya Sabha), Rashtriya Janata Dal

Salman Khurshid is not given to bombast or hyperbole. His are grounded narratives close to the ground, at times partisan but never prejudiced. The Congress leader's latest book, *Contesting Democratic Deficit*, co-authored with Mritunjay Singh Yadav, is in the same genre—scholarly, anecdotal and believable. It's a simply told story by an erudite lawyer-politician known for his understatement on a terrain crowded by loudmouths.

Vinod Sharma, political editor, *Hindustan Times*

In India's seventy-fifth constitutional year, the eighteenth Lok Sabha election brought back constitutional democracy from the brink of fascism. The BJP's previous majoritarian majority had undermined democratic principles and institutions pushed Muslims out of the democratic imagination. The voters, defying all predictions, denied the BJP a clear majority and created a fighting space for the opposition. *Contesting Democratic Deficit* by Congress leader Salman Khurshid with Mritunjay Singh Yadav details how the Congress and INDI Alliance strategized against the BJP hegemony. It analyses the election background, BJP's majoritarian campaign, Opposition response, institutional role, and parliamentary dynamics. This book is a sober account of the politics of the Congress party, its perception of the challenges faced by our democracy, its understanding of the election, and the implication of the results for our Republic's future.

Apoorvanand Jha, writer and professor, University of Delhi

CONTESTING DEMOCRATIC DEFICIT

An Inside Story of the 2024 Elections

SALMAN KHURSHID
with MRITUNJAY SINGH YADAV

Published by
Rupa Publications India Pvt. Ltd 2025
7/16, Ansari Road, Daryaganj
New Delhi 110002

Sales centres:
Bengaluru Chennai
Hyderabad Jaipur Kathmandu
Kolkata Mumbai Prayagraj

Copyright © Salman Khurshid with Mritunjay Singh Yadav 2025

The views and opinions expressed in this book are the authors' own and the facts are as reported by them; these have been verified to the extent possible, and the publishers are not in any way liable for the same.

All rights reserved.
No part of this publication may be reproduced, transmitted, or stored in a retrieval system, in any form or by any means, electronic, mechanical, photocopying, recording or otherwise, without the prior permission of the publisher.

P-ISBN: 978-93-6156-356-0
E-ISBN: 978-93-6156-739-1

First impression 2025

10 9 8 7 6 5 4 3 2 1

The moral right of the authors has been asserted.

Printed in India

This book is sold subject to the condition that it shall not, by way of trade or otherwise, be lent, resold, hired out, or otherwise circulated, without the publisher's prior consent, in any form of binding or cover other than that in which it is published.

CONTENTS

Introduction When Symbolism Meets Conviction / vii

One The Lost Decade / 1

Two Bharat Jodo Yatra: The Voice of Bharat Mata / 33

Three India: Uniting to Defend the Idea of India / 49

Four A New Era of Campaigning / 61

Five Fighting the Politics of Falsehood / 95

Six The Mandate and the Message / 123

Epilogue New Politics on the Horizon / 159

Postscript Alliance Politics on the Brink: Navigating the Existential Crisis / 175

Index / 189

INTRODUCTION
WHEN SYMBOLISM MEETS CONVICTION

The ten years of the Narendra Modi government can be described in many ways. But nothing sums up the political conundrum better than the entry of the freshly elected leader who, each time after three successive elections, goes to a strategically placed original copy of the Constitution and reverentially lifts it to his bowed head. On the other hand, the Leader of Opposition (LoP) in the Lok Sabha, Rahul Gandhi, goes from meetings, big and small, displaying a red pocket edition of the Constitution, seeking people's resolve to preserve and protect it. Symbolism and conviction met head-on in the eighteenth Lok Sabha elections.

The last ten years since the BJP-NDA government came to power were portrayed as India's salvation and supposed release from the constraints of the past decades since Independence. Jawaharlal Nehru and his legacy, cherished by many, were under sustained attack, presumably in the expectation that everything else that flows from it would diminish in turn. For the Congress party and liberal India, it was a dark decade with periodic sparks of hope that said all was not lost.

As 2024 dawned, speculation began about the possible date of elections, keeping in mind the likely schedule for the inauguration of the Ram Temple in Ayodhya. Ram Janmabhoomi has taken centre stage over the ten years of the NDA rule and certainly since the Supreme Court judgement in 2019. The government seemed to have carefully worked out the timeline for the inauguration in January 2024. The occasion displayed nationwide approval and allegiance through flags and posters. Ahead of the much-awaited *Pran Pratishtha* at the Ram Temple, the Bharatiya Janata Party (BJP) faced resistance from top Sanatana Dharma spiritual leaders for rushing the temple's inauguration before it was complete.[1]

---

[1] 'Who are the four Shankaracharyas who rejected Ayodhya Ram Mandir invite and why are they unhappy with it? Explained', *Livemint*, 12 January 2024, https://tinyurl.com/bdenhnhv. Accessed on 19 December 2024.

Four Shankaracharyas decided not to be a part of the inauguration ceremony of the temple. Most of them expressed their displeasure that the ceremony did not follow the rules of Sanatana Dharma. Nevertheless, a massive gathering of eminent personalities from across the country were in attendance.

The reaction of the Congress party was closely watched. The polite rejection of the invitation caused a flutter among a few people, but generally, it was agreed that the event was a BJP-dominated one and the faithful would find their moment to pay obeisance. However, the Uttar Pradesh unit, led by President Ajay Rai and General Secretary Avinash Pandey, paid a visit before the inauguration date lest they be accused of neglecting Bhagwan Ram.

The BJP gave everyone the impression that the 2024 election was virtually sealed on the inauguration day, as homes and shops across the country donned the saffron colour. That it was not to be, as democracy claimed its own space. The result has made apparent that Indian democracy is sensitive to religion and takes note of it but does not cede control to it. Lawyers describe this as constitutional morality.

The 2024 general elections were long-drawn-out, in seven phases from 19 April to 1 June, with results on 4 June. Towards the end of that period, political and ambient temperatures had risen greatly. Political parties kept the Election Commission of India (ECI) busy by complaining about what their opponents said and did. In many of these complaints, the ECI acted promptly to the satisfaction of its interlocutors, but in many cases directly involving the incumbent prime minister, there was understandable embarrassment and blatant procrastination. They found a way to do this via media by directing their responses to the heads of the political parties instead of the person complaining about them. I am unsure if any specific utterance of PM Modi was even mildly castigated or shown displeasure.[2]

In the Indian political system, the prime minister and the chief minister are seldom seen as first among equals, unlike the Whitehall system of parliamentary democracy. Of course, there are exceptions, particularly in coalition politics, where this proposition is often qualified by the inclusion of a deputy leader as well as shared tenures. However, PM Modi can be said to be a powerful personification of this proposition. The work of an incumbent is usually described in the name of the head of government. But in the case of PM Modi, every government scheme displays his photo, bags of ration, or whatever. Even the COVID-19 vaccination certificate carries his photo.[3]

Not surprisingly, the 2024 general election was all about him, which means that any decline in support must inevitably be laid at his door. An incisive analysis by *The Quint* underscored the fatigue in Brand Modi: out of 164 constituencies where Prime Minister Narendra Modi had actively campaigned, delivering impassioned speeches, BJP and NDA candidates suffered defeats in 77 seats. This marked a significant decline from the 2019 Lok Sabha elections, where PM Modi's campaign trail had proved immensely successful, securing victories in 85 per cent of the constituencies he had visited.[4] In the 2024 elections, however, the BJP managed to secure a win in only 53 per cent of the seats where PM Modi's presence was felt, reflecting a notable

---

[2] Dahiya, Himanshi, '27 Cases, 1 Notice, No Action: What Did EC Do on Complaints Against PM Modi?', *The Quint*, 27 April 2024, https://tinyurl.com/4yss8t3s. Accessed on 15 January 2025.

[3] Pandey, Geeta, 'Narendra Modi: "Why is the Indian PM's photo on my Covid vaccine certificate?"', *BBC*, 19 October 2021, https://tinyurl.com/yrh55cxn. Accessed on 15 January 2025.

[4] Ibid.

reduction in electoral impact.[5] State-level analyses offer deeper insights into these national trends. With its record 31 rallies, Uttar Pradesh became a focal point where the 'Modi effect' faltered noticeably.[6] Despite the extensive campaigning, the BJP faced substantial losses, notably yielding ground to the resurgent Samajwadi Party (SP), which achieved historic highs in the state. In Maharashtra, PM Modi's 18 rallies did not translate into favourable outcomes for the NDA, as defeats were recorded in 15 of these constituencies.[7] Similarly, in West Bengal, where PM Modi held 23 public meetings and roadshows spanning 27 Lok Sabha constituencies, the BJP experienced setbacks, losing 20 seats.[8] PM Modi's re-election from Varanasi was tough, with his opponent, Ajay Rai of the Congress, leading for several rounds. There was no dramatic upset in the end, but the margin of victory was reduced to 1.52 lakh votes. In the 2019 Lok Sabha elections, PM Modi won the polls by a margin of 674,664 votes (63.6 per cent), while in the 2014 Lok Sabha polls, he won by a margin of 581,022 votes (56.4 per cent).[9] BJP and NDA candidates suffered defeats in 77 seats.[10]

These electoral dynamics prompted critical reflections on the evolving voter sentiments and regional political dynamics, challenging assumptions about enduring political charisma and its electoral sway in the diverse and dynamic Indian states.

---

[5] "Elections Results Show that "Modi Fatigue" Has Replaced the "Modi Bump"", *The Wire*, 7 June 2024, https://tinyurl.com/yc4x5fvz. Accessed on 11 November 2024.
[6] Ibid.
[7] Ibid.
[8] Ibid.
[9] 'Varanasi Lok Sabha Election results 2024', *The Times of India*, https://tinyurl.com/yc2zucx6. Accessed on 21 October 2024.
[10] Khan, Fatima, 'BJP and NDA Lost In Nearly Half The Seats Where PM Narendra Modi Held Rallies', *The Quint*, 5 June 2024, https://tinyurl.com/mv8rpadu. Accessed on 11 November 2024.

Contesting Democratic Deficit is a quickly produced version of an insider's view of the general election and therefore, obviously, must centre around the Congress party's view of the world in 2024. Many insiders and party leaders were assigned specific responsibilities, volunteers from universities for the war rooms, staff officers of senior leaders, members of the All India Congress Committee (AICC) departments, especially the Communications Department, the legal team handling election-related matters, et al. We have tried to share their experiences to the extent possible in the time available. In due course, the records will be available and election experts will analyze the election strategies and outcomes in detail. Hopefully, some critical markers will be provided by the narrative here.

The fervour, polemic and passion in the face-off during elections, particularly in a divisive and polarized atmosphere, resonates in reporting to some extent. However, taking the cue from our leader, Rahul Gandhi, we must be conscious that *nafrat ke bazaar mey mohabbat ki dukan kholni hai* (we have to set up a shop of love in a market of hatred). Furthermore, since PM Modi remains the dominant face of the political rival, the emotional element remains unsettled. One hoped that the fresh term of the government would start on a positive note, but the first few days in Parliament suggested the opposite. Be that as it may, with an enhanced presence and the Opposition led by Rahul Gandhi, there will be no bulldozing of the government's agenda, and inevitably, attempts to seek cooperation and consensus will be made.

In being critical of the government of the day, one must be conscious that anything said about it in the digitally connected world village also sticks to India's image. The obligation to speak out against any wrong cannot be overlooked either. Thus, an objective balance has guided this effort. The contest between hatemongers and advocates of love clearly cannot resort to hate to fortify the latter. It is a Gandhian quest, admirably portrayed in the play 'Shrivings' by Peter Shaffer.[11]

The dilemma of pacifists in dealing with individuals who resort to violent means to challenge the commitment to non-violence has remained a constant theme, as portrayed in the play. Inevitably, the conundrum of 'turning the other cheek' and 'eye for an eye will make the world blind' surfaces with the dilemma. Intuition and instinct, if not nurturing and genes, are said to be relevant influencers of our attitudes. But of course the thesis is far from concluded. The arguments to repudiate violence are available from the lives and works of Mahatma Gandhi, Nelson Mandela, and many others who have kept the flame of non-violence alive.

---

[11]Shrivings is the Cotswold home of Sir Gideon Petrie, an ageing, respected guru figure dedicated to non-violence who has turned this ancient retreat into a home for transients. His 'family' of active proteges and potential disciples is a young woman and a young man. The girl is a vegetarian veteran protestor preoccupied with commitment. The boy is a drop-out, over-eager and uncertain, finding half fulfilment in carpentry and superficial courting of the girl. The cement binding the trio is the worship of Gideon's noble ideal of total non-violence spiced with a dash of showmanship. The result is a fragile garden of Eden. Mark Askelon, the Philistine, arrives. A former pupil of Petrie who once worshipped his master's ideas, he has since forsaken them for more practical ones. His mission is to wreck his master's credo. Tortured by guilt and fuelled by liquor, his incapacity for immediate life forces him to experience life through others. He proposes a sadistic game using apples as buttons of original sin to shatter the unctuous facade of Shrivings and compel latent aggression to erupt in violence. The play ends with a Shaffer hallmark—a firm statement of love and human understanding.

ONE

THE LOST DECADE

The 2014 general election was a watershed in modern Indian politics, sweeping away the decades of dominance by the Indian National Congress.[1] The arrival of Prime Minister Narendra Modi was to change the ideological content of politics and the style of administration. Two versions of India emerged very quickly—one in the government that sought to reclaim the cultural edifice from illegitimate occupiers and the second in the alternative idea of an India committed to an inclusive character and a liberal intellectual ethos.

Curiously, many political entities and their allies had worked to undermine the Congress-United Progressive Alliance (UPA) government, compounded by a series of adverse judicial decisions that unravelled accomplishments in several sectors, like coal mining and telecom.[2] The BJP's concerted political attacks and complete non-cooperation on several fronts of political functioning led to the narrative of policy paralysis and corruption. The 2004 dream team returned to power in 2009 but was severely damaged and fatigued. Unrelenting assault by a combination of populism by India Against Corruption, with clandestine support from Rashtriya Swayamsevak Sangh (RSS) cadres, sapped all energy from the party.[3]

Defeat came inevitably. While the then Opposition sought to undermine the accomplishments of the UPA, the public at large remained ambiguous about economic reform and refused to be weaned off the state-controlled economy and its comforts. The Ram Temple movement continued to gather steam, and the

---

[1] Indian National Congress (INC) will be referred simply as the Congress or the Congress party.
[2] Ganguly, Sumit, 'The UPA II: Looking Back, Looking Forward', *Heinrich Boll Stiftung*, 26 February 2014, https://tinyurl.com/boell-UPA. Accessed on 14 January 2025.
[3] Ahmed, Shabbir, 'RSS stage-managed Anna Hazare movement, says ex-India Against Corruption team member', *The New Minute*, 30 July 2023, https://tinyurl.com/5fn7ek9d. Accessed on 4 November 2024.

so-called Hindutva feeling continued to grow.

The year 2019 gave the BJP and Modi electoral approval for a second term and the Congress considerable anxiety over what was described by some as a permanent change in India's thinking, making the BJP the largest political party in the democratic world and the putative natural ruling party.

Despite the BJP's remarkable success, the test of a nation's success, however, should ultimately be in the total gross happiness of its people, even if there is no mathematical model to measure it. Of course, this is a sum of comfort felt in personal safety and security, satisfying employment or occupation, housing and educational opportunity. Along with creature comforts, a general and collective sense of wellbeing contribute to a nation's happiness. Above all, a divided nation or community cannot claim to be happy because the life of a nation lies in its collective growth. The decade of Modi's India was anything but happy despite the glamorous display of achievements.

The Congress and its partners in the Opposition have a take on the last ten years that varies dramatically from the self-certification of unbounded success that the incumbent government gives itself. Curiously, while the INDIA Alliance underscores the end of the undeclared emergency of the last few years, the BJP continues to harp on the 'emergency mindset' of the Congress, despite the long history of electoral victories of the Congress, including the defeat of the Janata government in 1980, and the fact that many parties that lined up against the Congress then are its partners now.[4] One need not be apologetic for the Emergency or allow it to cast a shadow over our present combative stance against the perversion of democratic rights. The Emergency was declared in

---

[4]'Those who imposed Emergency have no right to profess love for our Constitution: PM Modi', *The Hindu*, 25 June 2024, https://tinyurl.com/546wr3r5. Accessed on 19 December 2024.

extreme circumstances of civil unrest that went far beyond civil disobedience.[5] The people of India rejected the Emergency in 1977, but eighteen months later gave Indira Gandhi a thumping majority. Since then, several election victories should have settled the issue. The concern now is the undeclared emergency that subverts liberty in a virulent form.[6]

Decoding Anyay Kaal

In her 2024 interim budget speech on 1 February, Finance Minister Nirmala Sitharaman confidently emphasized the government's achievements and announced that the government would lay a White Paper on the House table 'to look at where we were then till 2014 and where we are now, only for the purpose of drawing lessons from the mismanagement of those years.'[7]

In response, the Congress party was quick to act. The announcement of a 'Black Paper' on the ten years of the Modi government was swiftly made.[8] A dedicated team, including Amitabh Dubey, Varun Santosh and others, began working on a war footing to prepare the document within an incredibly tight deadline of less than seven days. Fortunately, some groundwork had already been laid for the Karnataka elections, where a similar

---

[5]Roychowdhury, Adrija, 'Four reasons why Indira Gandhi declared Emergency', *The Indian Express*, 25 June 2018, https://tinyurl.com/emergency-Indira-gandhi. Accessed on 14 January 2025.

[6]"Congress chief slams Modi over 10 years of "undeclared Emergency"", *The Hindu*, 25 June 2024, https://tinyurl.com/4n8bwd68. Accessed on 4 November 2024.

[7]Ministry of Finance, *Government To Lay White Paper On Economy - Then And Now*, 1 February 2024, https://tinyurl.com/4av34hv5. Accessed on 4 November 2024.

[8]'Congress 'black paper' on 'Modi government's failures' focuses on unemployment and neglect of non-BJP States', *The Hindu*, 8 February 2024, https://tinyurl.com/4zv5ey58. Accessed on 4 November 2024.

document covering nine years of the Modi government had been prepared. This existing document served as a foundation, allowing the team to focus on updating and expanding the content.

Once the Black Paper was completed, the question of who should release the document arose. While some believed that Rahul Gandhi should be the one to launch it, Rahul himself suggested that the Congress President, Mallikarjun Kharge, would be the most appropriate person to do so. The suggestion was accepted, and the decision was made. On 8 February, the Black Paper titled '10 Saal Anyay Kaal 2014-2024' was officially launched by Kharge.[9] The document brought to light the manner in which the Modi government's ten years in power had devastated the country's economy, abetted crimes against women, and committed grave injustices against the minorities in the country. It was essentially a chargesheet of the BJP's *anyay* (injustice) during its decade in power.[10]

The Mirage of Modinomics

In this document, the Congress stated that the *Anyay Kaal* (period of injustice) witnessed the highest unemployment rate in 45 years. 'Total unemployment was one crore in 2012 but rose to about four crores in 2022. Ten lakh sanctioned central government posts remain unfilled. The unemployment rate for graduates and postgraduates is 33 per cent—one in three are looking unsuccessfully for a job. This is why engineers are becoming coolies and PhDs are applying for railway peon jobs. And this is also why two unemployed persons die of suicide every hour.'[11]

---

[9] '10 Saal Anyay Kaal 2014-2024', https://tinyurl.com/58m9wc2f. Accessed on 4 November 2024.
[10] Ibid.
[11] Ibid.

The plight of those lucky to be employed as labourers from 2014 to 2023 was marked by stagnating real wages, as reported by the Labour Bureau's Wage Rate Index. Economic indicators revealed clear declines in their earnings, reflecting broader challenges in the labour market.[12] Instead of jobs in the manufacturing or export sector, workers were pushed into contractual engagement or self-employment.

While jobless growth is an endemic problem of our economy, the regular source of state employment was severely compromised by exam paper leaks across the country, adding to a deep sense of frustration among young aspirants and enormous delays sapping the morale of an entire generation.

The Agnipath Scheme, supposedly introduced to reduce the average age of serving recruits in the Armed Forces and lessen the burden of pension, came as a shock to aspirants for regular service of 15–20 years. The refusal to include the batch of candidates at an advanced selection stage was even more distressing—they were kept waiting for final decisions due to COVID-19.[13] A short age relaxation was all that was required. The courts refused to intervene in what was considered a policy matter.[14]

The Black Paper argued that the price of crude oil in the world market had fallen by 21 per cent between May 2014 and February 2024—from over $100 to $79 per barrel, but fuel prices remained close to ₹100 per litre. This raised the cost of all

---

[12] Das, Arindam, and Jean Drèze, 'The problem of India's stagnant real wages', *Ideas for India*, https://tinyurl.com/3y799kyp. Accessed on 4 November 2024.
[13] 'Congress launches Jai Jawan scheme to aid 1.5 lakh youth rejected by Agnipath', *The Hindu*, 31 January 2024, https://tinyurl.com/Congress-Jai-Jawan. Accessed on 14 January 2025.
[14] Kohli, Tushar, 'Agnipath a policy decision, can't interfere, says Delhi High Court; dismisses petitions challenging the controversial scheme', *The Leaflet*, 28 February 2023, https://tinyurl.com/agnipath-Delhi-court. Accessed on 14 January 2025.

essential commodities. Blunders like demonetization and a poorly designed GST completely derailed the economy and destroyed job-generating small businesses.[15]

The COVID-19 pandemic exacerbated the hardships arising from these economic blunders, disproportionately affecting the labour class. The nationwide lockdown triggered a humanitarian crisis within four hours and disrupted the livelihoods of over four crore migrant workers. Lacking transportation arrangements, many were forced to undertake arduous journeys on foot over long distances. The sight of young children riding on luggage was truly heartrending. For weeks, they walked home with their families and survived only because of the UPA's MGNREGA scheme. While the government remained impervious, the ordinary people went all out to help with food and shelter. Only billionaires seemed to receive support from the Modi government through corporate benefits.[16]

Amid these dire circumstances, a glimmer of hope emerged with the rapid development of the AstraZeneca vaccine, branded as Covishield in India. This vaccine not only provided protection to millions of Indians but also played a crucial role in global immunization efforts. However, recent developments have cast a shadow over these achievements. Reports of worrying side effects in vaccinated individuals led to the withdrawal of the vaccine from circulation.[17] This turn of events underscored the complex interplay between public health challenges, scientific

---

[15]'10 Saal Anyay Kaal 2014-2024', https://tinyurl.com/58m9wc2f. Accessed on 4 November 2024.

[16]Manzar, Osama, 'The good, the bad, the ugly: What went wrong during India's Covid-19 response', *The Times of India*, 22 November 2021, https://tinyurl.com/ysxxkvcv. Accessed on 14 January 2025.

[17]'AstraZeneca withdraws COVID vaccine worldwide weeks after admitting rare side effects', *The Times of India*, 8 May 2024, https://tinyurl.com/y56256d9. Accessed on 4 November 2024.

advancements, and ethical considerations surrounding vaccine safety. This turbulent period serves as a poignant chapter in contemporary Indian history, highlighting the resilience of its people amid adversity and the critical intersections of health, economics and social justice.

Post Covid, the spectre of growing inequality loomed large, characterized by what economists termed a 'K-shaped economy'.[18] In a press conference, Rahul Gandhi held a placard depicting this economic divide's stark reality. Statistics painted a troubling picture: By 2024, India's top one per cent of income earners had come to control over 40 per cent of the nation's total wealth, a staggering increase from 12.5 per cent in 1980. Such a profound economic divide is unacceptable, especially as India strove to secure its position among the leading global economies. The discourse around this widening wealth gap echoed through policy circles and public debates, highlighting deep-seated concerns about social justice and economic fairness and reflecting the tensions between industrial growth and agricultural sustainability in India's developmental trajectory.

The issue of rising prices also took centre stage; findings from a Lokniti-CSDS survey revealed mounting concerns among voters. Before the recent election, only 20 per cent had expressed worry about inflation, but this figure surged to 30 per cent in the survey conducted during the elections.[19]

These economic woes reshaped the political landscape and posed formidable challenges for the governing parties striving

---

[18] Muralidharan, Sukumar, 'Indian economy's 'K-shaped' recovery shows the rich are thriving, while the poor struggle', *Frontline*, 30 November 2023, https://tinyurl.com/38evdsxh. Accessed on 19 December 2024.

[19] 'Modi's election disappointment was caused by these factors: Inflation, jobs & more: Survey', *The Economic Times*, 6 June 2024, https://tinyurl.com/Modi-inflation. Accessed on 14 January 2025.

to retain voter trust amid growing economic anxieties. Not surprisingly, the electoral aftermath painted a telling picture: The BJP suffered significant setbacks in rural areas, losing a third of its parliamentary constituencies there. Previously holding sway over 201 rural seats in the 543-member parliament, the BJP's influence dwindled to 126 seats after the extensive election.[20] The outcome underscored deep-seated discontent in rural communities, exacerbated by job shortages and the burden of high inflation.

Politics of Hatred and Polarization

The Congress pointed out that BJP leaders had openly spread hate and violence across India on grounds of caste and religion.

> Ministers have called for violence against minorities and garlanded mob lynching convicts. MPs and MLAs have supported rapists on communal lines, called for violence against minorities, assaulted Dalit women, and abused SCs, STs and OBCs. Hate speech has reached new peaks, while caste atrocities like Una and Hathras shame the nation. Caste discrimination has been institutionalized in higher education. The BJP has also attacked entire states and communities for political gain, such as protesting farmers. Meanwhile, Manipur burnt for nine months with the BJP CM spreading hate, but PM Modi remained silent.[21]

The incidence of communal riots in the states has subsided, giving credence to the thesis that riots are the handiwork of out-of-power rightist forces. Of late, it seems rioting has been replaced

---

[20] Thomas, Chris, et al., 'Rural vote fall cost India's Modi a decisive election win', *Reuters*, 7 June 2024, https://tinyurl.com/3vc3hfmc. Accessed on 3 December 2024.
[21] '10 Saal Anyay Kaal 2014-2024', https://tinyurl.com/58m9wc2f. Accessed on 4 November 2024.

by targeted violence like lynching and physical assaults. The Northeast Delhi riots of 2020 were, therefore, both an exception to the norm and a new technique of oppression. Dismayed by the remarkable and sustained protests across Delhi symbolized by Shaheen Bagh, instigators ventured onto the streets to stir up unrest and provoke reactions.[22] Some petty politicians used hate speech of the kind not known in the past. Sometimes this was done in police presence, without a word being said to restrain the speeches.[23] The riots broke out after the student protestors were chased onto the Jamia Millia Islamia campus, and in various parts of Delhi, groups clashed or people from nearby villages attacked homes in Northeast Delhi.

The major riots had their origin in Jaffrabad, in Northeast Delhi, where a sit-in by women against the Citizenship (Amendment) Act (CAA) 2019 was in progress on a stretch of the Seelampur–Jaffrabad–Maujpur road, virtually blocking it. On 23 February 2020, BJP leader Kapil Mishra publicly called for Delhi Police to clear the roads, failing which he threatened to 'hit the streets'.[24] The local DCP stood behind him in full riot gear as he spoke. After Mishra's ultimatum, violence erupted almost immediately.[25] Initially, Hindu and Muslim attacks were equally spontaneous and lethal. Most deaths were attributed to gunfire.[26] By 25 February,

---

[22] Swati, Shikha, and Anisha Reddy, 'Delhi Burning: A Timeline Of Anti-CAA Protests And Northeast Delhi Violence', *Outlook*, 24 February 2023, https://tinyurl.com/delhi-CAA-protests. Accessed on 14 January 2025.

[23] 'Minister Anurag Thakur gets EC notice over 'goli maaro' slogan at Delhi rally', *Hindustan Times*, 5 September 2020, https://tinyurl.com/Anurag-Thakur-slogan. Accessed 14 January 2025.

[24] 'The Roots of the Delhi Riots: A Fiery Speech and an Ultimatum', *The New York Times*, https://tinyurl.com/3dxrdem3. Accessed on 23 December 2024.

[25] Ibid.

[26] 'Donald Trump and Narendra Modi hug as Delhi burns', *The Economist*, 27 February 2020, https://tinyurl.com/2785nmcs. Accessed on 3 December 2024.

the balance had shifted. Rioters wearing helmets and carrying sticks, stones, swords, or pistols, and the saffron flags of Hindu nationalism entered Muslim neighbourhoods as the police stood by.[27][28] Chants were heard of *Jai Shri Ram*. In the neighbourhood of Shiv Vihar, Hindu rioters attacked Muslim houses and businesses for three days, often firebombing them with cooking gas cylinders and gutting them without resistance from the police.[29] In some instances, Muslims countered perceived threats by returning the violence. On 25 February, a Muslim mob approached a Hindu neighbourhood, throwing stones and Molotov cocktails and firing guns.[30] During this time, stories were also told of Sikh and Hindu families coming to the aid of besieged Muslims; in some neighbourhoods, religious communities cooperated in protecting themselves from violence.[31]

The Union Government swiftly characterized the violence as spontaneous. Delhi Police, directly overseen by the central government, moved into the area in strength on 26 February after the Delhi High Court ordered them to move injured victims to hospitals. National Security Adviser Ajit Doval visited the area; PM Modi appealed for peace on X (formerly Twitter).[32] Delhi

---

[27]Gettleman, Jeffrey, et al., 'How Delhi's Police Turned Against Muslims', *The New York Times*, https://tinyurl.com/284ph844. Accessed on 9 December 2024.
[28]Landrin, Sophie, 'India: New Delhi in the grip of violent inter-communal conflicts', *Le Monde*, 26 February 2020, https://tinyurl.com/ysuwdvkm. Accessed on 3 December 2024.
[29]Ellis-Petersen, Hannah, and Shaikh Azizur Rahman, '"I cannot find my father's body": Delhi's fearful Muslims mourn riot dead', *The Guardian*, 6 March 2020, https://tinyurl.com/25x4286j. Accessed on 3 December 2024.
[30]Slater, Joanna, and Niha Masih, 'What Delhi's worst communal violence in decades means for Modi's India', *The Washington Post*, https://tinyurl.com/4skrfwju. Accessed on 9 December 2024.
[31]'Delhi riots: 'Hero cop' who braved a mob to save lives', *BBC*, 28 February 2020, https://tinyurl.com/3cy3cxce. Accessed on 3 December 2024.
[32]'Victims of rioting in India are bashed by the police and courts, too',

Police was accused by the affected citizens, eyewitnesses, human rights organizations and Muslim leaders around the world of falling short in protecting Muslims.[33] Videos showed police acting in a coordinated manner against Muslims, occasionally helping Hindu gangs.[34]

Many Muslims were arrested and remain in custody, including student leaders.[35] Safoora Zargar, 28, was allegedly held in solitary confinement, denied regular contact with family, and not provided adequate medical care or diet. She was granted bail in her sixth month of pregnancy on humanitarian grounds.[36] The other ten jailed protesters were Meeran Haider, Gulfisha Fatima, Asif Iqbal Tanha, Devangana Kalita, Natasha Narwal, Khalid Saifi, Shifa Ur Rehman, Kafeel Khan, Sharjeel Imam, Umar Khalid and Akhil Gogoi.[37] Some were released by the High Court. Although the Supreme Court reversed the judgements, stating they would not be treated as precedents, the bails granted were not cancelled.[38] The 'provocative' speeches made during the sit-ins did not all incite violence but may have been offensive to the sober mind.

The Economist, 12 March 2020, https://tinyurl.com/Delhi-riots. Accessed on 3 December 2024.

[33] Frayer, Lauren, 'Delhi Riots Aftermath: "How Do You Explain Such Violence?"', *NPR*, 7 March 2020, https://tinyurl.com/ycx4zp98. Accessed on 3 December 2024.

[34] "How Delhi's Police Turned Against Muslims", *The New York Times*, https://tinyurl.com/yc4c58jc. Accessed on 3 December 2024.

[35] "Delhi 2020 religious riots: Amnesty International accuses police of rights abuses", *BBC*, 28 August 2020, https://tinyurl.com/2r6ct7zk. Accessed on 23 December 2024.

[36] "UN human rights experts urge India to release anti-CAA protesters", *Al Jazeera*, 26 June 2020, https://tinyurl.com/4pmh4e7u. Accessed on 23 December 2024.

[37] Ibid.

[38] "Delhi riots: SC refuses to stay bail granted to 3 activists, to examine HC order on anti-terror law", *The Times of India*, 18 June 2021, https://tinyurl.com/7kpdsev7. Accessed on 23 December 2024.

But there was no way that they could be described as anti-national or seditious. The Unlawful Activities (Prevention) Act (UAPA), imposed on many of the protagonists, led to their prolonged incarceration. Many still remain behind bars. Tukde Tukde Gang and Khan Market Gang are epithets wildly used for them, even sanctified by PM Modi himself.[39][40] Putting a political spin on these to gain electoral traction is one thing, but converting them into criminal proceedings is surreal. India and its unity are not so fragile as to collapse and fall apart due to speech histrionics emanating from youthful passion.

In a plural society, one must carefully watch areas of clash between communities and competing interests. Gurugram, the corporate capital and investment hub of North India in the vicinity of Delhi, has become a site of communal tension over *namaz* being held on Fridays in public parks. Staunch Hindu organizations have sought to prevent namaz gatherings with little cooperation from the local police to enforce rights. The Muslims who have moved to Gurugram are either upper-middle-class professionals or individuals from low-income groups, such as housemaids and class-four employees. There is no accommodation except shanties on encroached land which are periodically demolished. The land is not allotted for additional mosques to be built, and the few existing mosques have long passed their carrying capacity.[41]

---

[39]Deshpande Pandit, Vinaya, 'Congress run by *tukde tukde* gang, PM Modi says in Vidarbha', *The Hindu*, 20 September 2024, https://tinyurl.com/yc54jnzv. Accessed on 5 November 2024.

[40]Mohan, Archis, 'Spent their lives concealing sins of Cong: PM's jibe at "Khan Market gang"', *Business Standard*, 22 May 2024, https://tinyurl.com/bp7yauem. Accessed on 5 November 2024.

[41]Khalique Ahmed, Syed, 'Gurugram 'Namaz' Row: BJP Govt Refuses To Allot Land For Mosques, Not Removing Encroachment On 19 Mosques', *India Tomorrow*, 10 November 2021, https://tinyurl.com/gurugram-mosques. Accessed on 14 January 2025.

The nearby rural areas of Mewat remain trapped in educational and social backwardness and are unable to organize resistance to the violations of civil liberties in Gurugram. The rapid growth of urban areas and the stagnation of the rural areas have emerged as a contradiction of our modern existence, and a touch of communalism makes it a toxic combination. On 31 July 2023, communal violence erupted between Hindus and Muslims in the Nuh district of Haryana during an annual Braj Mandal Jalabhishek Yatra organized by the Vishva Hindu Parishad (VHP).[42] Reportedly, the Muslim community was angered when it was announced that the procession would include Bajrang Dal activist and cow vigilante Monu Manesar, who was wanted by the police as a suspect in the murder of two Muslim men; eventually though, the man did not show up at the procession. Upon hearing that Manesar would be in attendance, the local Muslim community organized an attack on the procession, pelting it with stones, bottles and Molotov cocktails.[43] This triggered retaliatory action from the Hindu procession participants. By the evening, fresh incidents of communal violence were reported from Gurugram and Sohna. The fatal assault on Maulana Saad, 22, the *Naib Imam* of Anjuman Jama Masjid in Gurugram's Sector 57, past midnight, when a mob of 90–100 Hindu vigilantes allegedly entered the mosque, set it ablaze, and killed him, as indeed an attack on homes have left a scar on the unblemished harmony of the area since Independence.[44] As

---

[42] Sushil, Manav, 'Nuh violence puts focus on Meo Muslims of Mewat—who they are & what is their history', *The Print*, 5 August 2023, https://tinyurl.com/5xkkvewu. Accessed on 23 December 2024.

[43] Jafri, Alishan, and Kaushik Raj, 'Who is Monu Manesar, Indian vigilante accused of inciting Haryana violence?', *Al Jazeera*, 14 August 2023, https://tinyurl.com/37ffxstv. Accessed on 23 December 2024.

[44] Taskin, Bismee, 'Shops burnt, imam killed, mosque torched—how Nuh clashes spawned targeted violence in Gurugram', *The Print*, 1 August 2023, https://tinyurl.com/3txtmuh8. Accessed on 23 December 2024.

of 3 August, the situation had resulted in at least seven fatalities and over 200 reported injuries.

It is, therefore, not surprising that the US State Department's International Religious Freedom Report for 2022, debunked by the government, expresses several concerns over India's religious freedom. It highlights that religious conversion is restricted in multiple states, that religious minorities are attacked on a regular basis, and that Muslims have alleged systemic discrimination—including 'cow vigilantism', which often results in attacks for alleged cow slaughter or beef trade.[45]

On diversity, other than paying lip service, there seems little effort to understand the implications. The issues that continue to hover on the horizon include the hijab ban in Karnataka, diluted by the split judgement of the Supreme Court but subsequently revived by a more recent decision of the Bombay High Court. If Sikhs can be permitted to dress according to their religious precepts without seriously compromising the commitment to equality in the prescribed dress, it is strange that wearing of hijab should be treated as an impermissible departure from the norm.

Although the BJP-led central government continues to profess its commitment to the Uniform Civil Code (UCC), the draft sought to be implemented in Uttarakhand, with lack of clarity on its implications, leaves many questions unanswered. The decision to abolish the Maulana Azad National Fellowship and merging minority scholarships with the general pool is another example of diluting targeted benefits. The policy on police encounters and demolition of houses continues to be a red rag for civil society but gets sporadic attention from courts.

◆

---

[45]'India 2022 International Religious Freedom Report', https://tinyurl.com/3ck93kzw.November 2024.

Crimes against Scheduled Caste (SC) and Scheduled Tribe (ST) communities increased by 48 per cent in 2022 compared to 2013. 'The government's refusal to hold the Socioeconomic and Caste Census to enumerate OBCs is an insult to those who are being denied representation in jobs and educational institutions because they are not being counted. Privatization and contractual engagement represent a twin attack on reservations, especially in critical sectors like health and education.'[46]

The government's inaction toward atrocities allowed humiliating conduct against Dalits,[47] causing tragedies like the suicide of University of Hyderabad scholar Rohith Vemula in January 2016.[48] His death sparked protests and outrage across India and gained widespread media attention as a case of state-sponsored discrimination against Dalits in Indian universities. However, the District Level Scrutiny Committee in Guntur district of Andhra Pradesh, which reviewed the Dalit status of Rohith Vemula, submitted its final report to the government in 2017 stating that neither Rohith nor his mother, Radhika, were Dalits. Nevertheless, previous incidents reveal a recurring pattern where upper-caste individuals have employed urination as a means to assert their superiority over lower castes. While other methods of dominance exist, the use of excreta and urine to dehumanize Dalits carries a distinctive arrogance.

♦

Yet another issue raised by the Congress was the surge in rape cases and injustice against women. 'A total of 31,516 rape cases

---

[46] '10 Saal Anyay Kaal 2014-2024', https://tinyurl.com/58m9wc2f. Accessed on 4 November 2024.
[47] '2022: A Look back at hate crimes against Dalits and Adivasis', *CJP*, 3 January 2023, https://tinyurl.com/hate-crime-India. Accessed on 14 January 2025.
[48] 'Shockwaves across Hyderabad Central Uni as Dalit student commits suicide, students angry', *The NEWS Minute*, 18 January 2016, https://tinyurl.com/Rohith-Vemula. Accessed on 14 January 2025.

were recorded in 2022 in India, with an average of 86 a day. While rapes are on the rise, the conviction rate stands at an abysmal 27.4 per cent. Whether it is Kuldeep Singh Sengar, the BJP MLA implicated in the Unnao rape [...] or the cover-up of the Hathras rape case, the BJP seems to stand for rapists against the victims.'[49]

In fact, this stand was reinforced in August 2022, when eleven men convicted and sentenced to life imprisonment for the gang rape of Bilkis Bano, a pregnant Muslim woman, during the 2002 Gujarat riots, were released on the grounds of 'good conduct' by the Gujarat government. The Modi government's Home Ministry had officially ratified the release order.[50] In a shocking display of insensitivity, the released convicts were garlanded and lauded for 'being Brahmins with good *sanskaar*' (values and ideals).[51] In January 2024, the Supreme Court struck down the release, and the matter was remanded to the Maharashtra government, in whose jurisdiction the trials had taken place.[52] It remains to be seen how the Supreme Court's direction will be observed in letter and spirit.

◆

The saga of the farmers' protests against the contentious farm laws unfolded as another turbulent chapter in recent history, marked by tragedy and widespread unrest. Over the course of the protests, which spanned several months starting from November 2020,

---

[49]Ibid.
[50]'India's Modi government approved release of Bilkis Bano's rapists', *Al Jazeera*, 18 October 2022, https://tinyurl.com/4uj7ur2m. Accessed on 5 November 2024.
[51]'Bilkis Bano's Rapists Are "Brahmins, Have Good Sanskar": BJP MLA', *NDTV*, 18 August 2022, https://tinyurl.com/2s4fwx2m. Accessed on 5 November 2024.
[52]Shamim, Sarah, 'How did India's Supreme Court send Bilkis Bano's rapists back to jail?', *Al Jazeera*, 9 January 2024, https://tinyurl.com/ydktbu76. Accessed on 5 November 2024.

approximately 750 farmers tragically lost their lives, reflecting the immense toll of the movement.[53]

The protests reached a tragic climax in October 2021 with the shocking incident in Lakhimpur Kheri district where a convoy of three SUVs, including one owned by the former Minister of State for Home Affairs Ajay Mishra, allegedly mowed down and killed eight people.[54] This incident sparked nationwide outrage and intensified the calls for justice and accountability.

In a dramatic turn of events, Priyanka Gandhi Vadra was detained at a guest house in Sitapur while attempting to meet the families of the victims, further galvanizing public sentiment against the handling of the protests.[55]

Amid renewed marches towards Delhi, the protests turned deadly once more. Shubhkaran Singh from Punjab's Baloke village met his untimely demise in a clash between security forces and protesting farmers at the Khanauri border. Darshan Singh died of cardiac arrest amid the fervour of the demonstrations. Gyan Singh from Gurdaspur, along with Manjeet Singh and Narendra Pal Singh, also tragically passed away during the protests, highlighting the human cost of the unrest. This period of unrest and tragedy underscored the profound socioeconomic and political challenges facing India's agricultural sector, prompting urgent calls for dialogue, reform and justice in the aftermath of the protests.

---

[53]'750 Died During Farmers Protest, No Condolence From Centre: Farmer Leader', *NDTV*, 8 November 2021, https://tinyurl.com/India-farmer-protest. Accessed on 14 January 2025.
[54]Sahu, Manish, and Asad Rehman, 'Minister's car runs over 4 protesters in Lakhimpur Kheri, farmers blame son; 4 more die in violence', *Indian Express*, 4 October 2021, https://tinyurl.com/2s3875kv. Accessed on 4 November 2024.
[55]'Lakhimpur Kheri: Priyanka Gandhi arrested, Sitapur guest house turned into temporary jail', *India Today*, 5 October 2021, https://tinyurl.com/vxw55c4k. Accessed on 23 December 2024.

The political fallout was significant, particularly in the northern states, where the BJP faced electoral setbacks. The Centre for the Study of Developing Societies (CSDS), through its Lokniti survey, noted that the anger and grievances of the farmers resonated deeply with voters, influencing political dynamics in the northern states.[56]

From the agricultural fields, the protests moved to the sports field. In January 2023, the uproar began at Jantar Mantar, where Indian wrestlers—led by prominent names including Vinesh Phogat, Bajrang Punia and Sakshi Malik—voiced allegations of sexual exploitation and intimidation against Wrestling Federation of India (WFI) chief Brij Bhushan Sharan Singh. Their demands for his resignation and the dissolution of the WFI echoed in the protests. As tensions escalated, the wrestlers attempted to march towards the new parliament building that was inaugurated by PM Modi. However, their actions led to charges of rioting and obstruction of public servants.[57] Both the International Olympic Committee (IOC) and United World Wrestling (UWW) condemned the handling and detention of the athletes by the local authorities, denouncing it as deeply concerning.[58] In a dramatic turn of events, the wrestlers travelled to Haridwar, where they stopped short of immersing their international medals in the Ganga, making a powerful statement against the perceived injustices.

Meanwhile, the UWW took decisive action, suspending

---

[56]Gupta, Vivek, 'Farmers' Anger Hurt the BJP in Several Northern States: CSDS-Lokniti Survey', *The Wire*, 22 June 2024, https://tinyurl.com/ms9pfytr. Accessed on 4 November 2024.
[57]'Wrestlers' protest: Vinesh Phogat, Sakshi Malik, Bajrang Punia booked after scuffle with Delhi Police', *Business Today*, 29 May 2023, https://tinyurl.com/5fhmeap8. Accessed on 23 December 2024.
[58]'IOC condemns police action against wrestlers, urges IOA to protect athletes', *National Herald*, 1 June 2023, https://tinyurl.com/ymz8azpj. Accessed on 23 December 2024.

WFI for failing to conduct timely elections. Amidst the turmoil, Sanjay Singh, a staunch supporter of Brij Bhushan, emerged as the new WFI chief. This development prompted Sakshi Malik to announce her retirement from wrestling in protest, while Bajrang Punia returned his prestigious Padma Shri award as a gesture of defiance against Singh's controversial election.[59][60]

India found itself in the throes of a multifaceted crisis when, in September 2023, the G20 Summit was portrayed by PM Modi as a special accomplishment of the leader.

The truth was that it was India's turn by sequence. Most countries put their best foot forward, and the extensive advertisements and hoardings across the country were no exception. However, the slums of Delhi were carefully hidden behind sheets for the G20 delegates, as was done even earlier during US President Donald Trump's visit in 2020. In the latter's case, the forced evictions from NRC-CAA protest sites caused deep unrest and distortion of law.

With so much wrong happening, sections of society began to break out of their suspension of disbelief and ask questions, often in private. The discontent spilled over at times, like the Shaheen Bagh sit-in by the *dadi*s (grandmothers), the several month-long *dharna*s of farmers, and the protests by women athletes, though large-scale nationwide movements seen in the heyday of the JP movement were not replicated. No one can tell how long it will take to explode. What is clear, however, is that the incumbent government seems very concerned about the long-term impact

---

[59]'Bajrang Punia writes to PM Modi, says he is returning Padma Shri in protest', *The Hindu,* 23 December 2023, https://tinyurl.com/2tcsudby. Accessed on 14 January 2025.

[60]'Sakshi Malik says she won't compete under presidency of Brij Bhushan loyalist', *The Times of India,* 21 December 2023, https://tinyurl.com/muzxpffa. Accessed on 14 January 2025.

of the simmering anger and frustration on our society, already struggling with the growing incidence of crime.

Democracy's Darkest Days

Bureaucratic suspicion of civil society has always been prevalent under successive governments. The fear, real or imagined, of the 'foreign hand' has haunted people in high places. But, under the UPA-I, many traditional barricades were brought down. The National Advisory Council (NAC) was a major new dimension of policymaking, headed by UPA Chairperson Sonia Gandhi, and included some outstanding civil society representatives. Along with a refurbished Planning Commission under Dr Montek Singh Ahluwalia, they took innovative initiatives for welfare measures and better governance.

Among these far-sighted schemes was the Mahatma Gandhi National Rural Employment Guarantee Act, 2005 (MGNREGA). Since the outset of his tenure, PM Modi, who described the scheme as a living tribute to the UPA government's failure, had expressed reservations about its long-term efficacy.[61] Yet, during the government's tenure, the issue of nonpayment of dues under MGNREGA emerged as a persistent concern. Reports indicated that states were owed approximately ₹6,366 crore, highlighting systemic challenges within the rural employment programme.[62] PM Modi's administration viewed the terms of trade as favouring industry over agriculture, posing challenges to the agricultural

---

[61]'Modi says MNREGA will continue as a living monument to Congress failure', *Scroll.in*, 27 February 2015, https://tinyurl.com/4hmaf944. Accessed on 14 January 2025.
[62]'Centre owes Rs 6,366 crore in dues to states under MGNREGS', *Scroll.in*, 2 August 2023, https://tinyurl.com/MGNREGS-Centre. Accessed on 14 January 2025.

sector's sustainability. In response, the Congress party had advocated for measures aimed at addressing these disparities. It proposed enhanced compensation for land acquisition, improvements in the minimum support prices (MSP) for agricultural produce, and strengthened provisions under the Employment Guarantee Scheme. Despite these efforts, subsequent governments undermined these initiatives, leading to ongoing issues such as delayed payments and inadequate support for rural employment.

Even as *Vishwa Bandhu* (friend of the world) was making friends across the globe, it resiled from *Athiti Satkaar* (guest hospitality) at home. The NAC was disbanded, and so was the Planning Commission. Next to be targeted were iconic civil society groups whose funds were cut off under the Foreign Contribution (Regulation) Act. The Enforcement Directorate (ED) and the Central Bureau of Investigation (CBI) were unleashed on them.[63]

While the successor government undermined certain schemes, it renamed some existing laws to claim the benefits. The Bharatiya Nyaya Sanhita 2023 replacing the Indian Penal Code 1860 (IPC), the Bharatiya Nagarik Suraksha Sanhita 2023 replacing the Criminal Procedure Code 1973 (CrPC), and the Bharatiya Sakshya Adhiniyam 2023 replacing the Indian Evidence Act 1872 (IEA), received the assent of the President of India on 25 December 2023 and came into effect on 1 July 2024, soon after the elections.

The wholesome amendments were made without advice from the Law Commission or scrutiny of Parliamentary Committees. No legal advice was sought from criminal law experts, academics

---

[63]Rajalakshmi, T.K., 'Modi government's crackdown on FCRA cripples civil society organisations', *Frontline*, 3 February 2024, https://tinyurl.com/Modi-FCRA. Accessed on 14 January 2025.

or practitioners.⁶⁴ ⁶⁵ The general trend of the new laws shows little evidence of reform that is citizen-centric, that liberalizes oppressive provisions or decriminalizes outdated concepts.

Apart from changing the names of IPC, CrPC and IEA to the Hindi versions, sections of the acts have been indiscriminately swapped around, apart from additions that make the laws more stringent and taxing for citizens. Much of the beneficial interpretation of penal provisions may no longer have binding force as the text has been altered. For months on end, lawyers and judges, not to mention litigants, will be forced to steer through unfamiliar territory, adding to the misery of criminal proceedings.

> Under the Anyay Kaal, all checks and balances have been diluted, and institutions turned into rubber stamps. All independent institutions of the country—judiciary (said with greatest respect and care), election commission, RBI, media critical to maintaining a robust democracy stand compromised and subverted.'⁶⁶ 'Elected state governments in Arunachal Pradesh, Goa, Karnataka, Madhya Pradesh, Maharashtra and Manipur were undermined after the BJP used blatant money power and threats of investigation to induce MLAs to switch sides. Since 2014, a 5-fold jump in ED cases against politicians has occurred; 95 per cent of these politicians are from the Opposition.⁶⁷

---

[64] Kumar, Suresh, 'Centre could have consulted law panel before bringing in new criminal laws: Madras HC', *The Times of India*, 20 July 2024, https://tinyurl.com/criminal-laws-Madras-HC. Accessed on 14 January 2025.
[65] Rajalakshmi, T.K., 'New criminal laws expand police powers and restrict civil liberties', *Frontline*, 21 July 2024, https://tinyurl.com/criminal-laws-civil-liberties. Accessed 14 January 2024.
[66] '10 Saal Anyay Kaal 2014-2024', https://tinyurl.com/58m9wc2f. Accessed on 4 November 2024.
[67] Ibid.

Investigations have been initiated even after elections are announced, and the Model Code of Conduct has kicked in.

During parliamentary sessions, BJP Members of Parliament (MPs) received more camera time while speaking, often overshadowing their opponents. The microphones of Opposition MPs were frequently muted.[68] Ramesh Bidhuri, a BJP MP, used hurtful communal language in the Lok Sabha for Danish Ali, then a Bahujan Samaj Party (BSP) member. Rahul Gandhi met Danish Ali to express solidarity after Bidhuri's attack. Yet nothing came of the notices issued to both the victim and the attacker. The BSP suspended Danish Ali from the party.[69] He subsequently contested from Amroha on a Congress ticket.

The suspension of 146 MPs from both houses of Parliament during the 2023 Winter Session was a sad moment in the history of our parliamentary democracy. In addition, the House membership of Rahul Gandhi (over conviction in a defamation case) and Mahua Moitra (after the findings of the Ethics Committee) was terminated, with notices to vacate their respective residences coming on the heels. The stirring image of a young girl reaching out to Rahul Gandhi and offering him her home remains etched in the mind. While the Supreme Court overturned Rahul's termination, Mahua's was overturned by voters in the 2024 parliamentary election.[70] The country needs to reflect on these episodes and their impact on the nature of our democracy.

---

[68] 'Lok Sabha Speaker vs Opposition over 'muting' of mics: Who controls them in Parliament?', *Firstpost*, 1 July 2024, https://tinyurl.com/2v25svx3. Accessed 14 January 2025,

[69] 'BJP member Ramesh Bidhuri uses communal remarks in Lok Sabha', *The Hindu*, 23 September 2023, https://tinyurl.com/36ay45xb. Accessed on 23 December 2024.

[70] 'Parliament Winter Session 2023 highlights: Mahua Moitra's expulsion, security breach, suspension of 146 MPs', *The Indian Express*, 22 December 2023, https://tinyurl.com/y9dwbj22. Accessed on 23 December 2024.

Not giving space to Opposition parliamentarians is dwarfed by the hijacking of political outfits and unseating of elected governments—the Maharashtra saga of breaking up the Shiv Sena and NCP, the Goa government formation, unsettling Kamal Nath's government in Madhya Pradesh, and interfering with the stability of the Himachal Pradesh government of chief minister Sukhvinder Singh Sukhu are just a few instances.

The BJP has effectively become a 'political washing machine', where politicians once targeted under the amended Prevention of Money-Laundering Act (PMLA), particularly Section 50 (2), find themselves absolved of scrutiny upon joining the party. Politicians facing charges under the PMLA often emerge with their reputations cleansed, their past allegations seemingly forgotten, and their records untarnished. Many people cutting across sectors were put in the dock, but Jharkhand Chief Minister Hemant Soren and former chief minister of Delhi Arvind Kejriwal were arrested while Kejriwal was still in office, writing a black chapter in the history of the government.

There are major issues of public policy involved here. No one rejects accountability in high places, but the need to arrest in such cases is seldom justified, smacking of political vendetta. This is particularly apparent in the case of people who escape the dragnet of the ED and CBI because of affiliations with the ruling party or their connections. The unimaginable has become commonplace, turning India into a nation of prisoners. Ironically, P. Chidambaram, the author of the PMLA, was himself taken into custody and imprisoned for several weeks before being granted bail. Unfortunately, the Supreme Court could not be persuaded to intervene urgently and attempts to seek immediate relief became infructuous because of the arrest.[71]

---

[71]Choudhary, Shrimi, 'INX Media case: ED arrests Chidambaram; to produce him in PMLA court today', *Business Standard*, 16 October 2019,

To address the endemic problem of political finance and make it transparent, the Electoral Bonds Scheme 2018 was introduced. From the beginning, there were doubts about how the bonds would affect the level-playing field. The bonds were introduced with two objectives: reducing corruption and bribery by keeping donors anonymous, and bringing transparency to campaign funding by routing all donations through legitimate banking channels. The promise was that anonymity would protect donors from potential reprisals while fostering transparency in political donations. However, investigative journalist Poonam Agarwal, working for *The Quint*, exposed a startling truth: While the names of donors were kept hidden from the public and opposition parties, the government secretly tracked each donor using a hidden unique alphanumeric code embedded in the bonds visible only under ultraviolet light.[72] This revelation not only undermined the promise of transparency but also exposed a covert mechanism of control, where the government had full knowledge of who was contributing, further fuelling concerns of quid pro quo arrangements between corporations and the ruling party.

Reports of large donations filling the ruling party's coffers confirmed the worst fears. The matter reached the Supreme Court, and orders were passed for disclosure. The nexus between the donors and government, donors and investigative agencies was laid bare, as was the extent of contributions to different parties, disproportionately to the BJP.

On 15 February 2024, the Supreme Court unanimously struck down the Electoral Bonds Scheme. The Bench held that the Scheme violated the voters' right to information enshrined in

---

https://tinyurl.com/Chidambaram-arrested. Accessed on 14 January 2025.
[72] Agarwal, Poonam, 'How The Quint's Poonam Agarwal Exposed Hidden Numbers on Electoral Bonds', *The Quint*, 19 March 2024, https://tinyurl.com/3etkbrtv. Accessed on 7 November 2024.

Article 19(1)(a) of the Constitution. The court also directed that the sale of electoral bonds be stopped with immediate effect. The State Bank of India (SBI) was directed to submit to the ECI the details of the electoral bonds purchased from 12 April 2019 to date. This was to include details of the purchaser as well as the political parties to whom the bonds were given. Further, the court ordered the ECI to publish the information shared by the SBI on its official website within a week of receiving the information (by 13 March 2024). But of course there was no further order to disgorge the large amounts secured by the ruling party.[73]

The ECI's avowed efforts to provide a level-playing field remain stillborn given the huge funds disparity between the ruling party and the Opposition. If that was not bad enough, the Income Tax Department moved in to freeze Congress party's bank accounts on the eve of the elections.[74]

The scrutiny of the Congress party's finances came in the wake of inexplicable questioning of top party leaders, including Sonia Gandhi and Rahul Gandhi, by the ED for the *National Herald's* Young India Limited, for several hours in 2022. Purported intimidation and harassment could have been the sole motive that prompted Rahul to enthuse the party cadres with his *Daro Mat* message.[75]

◆

There was much noise about Pegasus in 2021, but an impervious government stonewalled and carried on business as usual. Pegasus

---

[73] 'Supreme Court strikes down Electoral Bonds Scheme for being violative of right to information under Art. 19(1)(a) of Constitution', *SCC Online*, 15 February 2024, https://tinyurl.com/236xw9hm. Accessed on 11 November 2024.
[74] 'Income Tax department freezes bank accounts of Congress; Ajay Maken says, "no money to pay bills or salary"', *Mint*, 16 February 2024, https://tinyurl.com/Congress-accounts-freeze. Accessed 14 January 2025.
[75] '"Daro Mat" should become the Congress war cry: Tushar Gandhi', *National Herald*, 23 February 2023, https://tinyurl.com/3dn4wn36. Accessed on 11 November 2024.

is a spyware developed by the Israeli cyber-arms company NSO Group that is designed to be covertly and remotely installed on mobile phones running iOS and Android. While NSO Group markets Pegasus as a product for fighting crime and terrorism, governments around the world have routinely used spyware to surveil journalists, lawyers, political dissidents and human rights activists. The Israeli defence ministry must approve the sale of Pegasus licenses to foreign governments.

As of March 2023, Pegasus operators could remotely install the spyware on iOS versions through 16.0.3 using a zero-click exploit. While the capabilities of Pegasus may vary over time due to software updates, it is generally capable of reading text messages, call snooping, collecting passwords, location tracking, accessing the target device's microphone and camera, and harvesting information from apps. Several important public persons have received a warning from Apple about their phones being under Pegasus surveillance.[76]

As a result, the country's atmosphere has become worrying. People leave their homes to talk about sensitive subjects; most telephonic conversations are made via WhatsApp. The big-brother syndrome has hit the mainstream media hard but talk of widespread snooping is common. We are fast becoming a country of thieves and paranoia. The over-the-shoulder posture of the citizen does not preserve the democratic ambience.

Hartosh Singh Bal, the executive editor at *The Caravan*, reiterated how PM Modi quickly realized the institutional weaknesses of India's mainstream media, leading to its alignment with centralized authority.[77] The media landscape was dramatically

---

[76]"Several politicians get Apple's alert on their phones being targeted by State-sponsored attackers', *Business Line*, 31 October 2023, https://tinyurl.com/Apple-alerts. Accessed 14 January 2025.

[77]Dutta, Anisha, 'Small signs of hope—but a long way to go—for Indian media independence', *Columbia Journalism Review*, https://tinyurl.com/mryxzch3. Accessed on 11 November 2024.

altered in December 2022 when the Adani Group, led by billionaire Gautam Adani, announced control of nearly 65 per cent of New Delhi Television (NDTV), a prominent and critical voice in Indian journalism. The hostile takeover bid marked the end of NDTV's critical coverage, occurring without any input or consent from its founders. Reporters voiced concern, emphasizing that media acquisitions by oligarchs threatened pluralistic public debate in India.[78] Despite initial assurances, the Adani takeover quickly altered NDTV's editorial stance.

The aftermath saw prominent journalists like Ravish Kumar, Sreenivasan Jain and Nidhi Razdan leave NDTV, significantly changing the organization's management and editorial line. Razdan noted that NDTV was the last television news channel holding power accountable.[79]

Not surprisingly, in the fraught landscape of Indian journalism, 2024 stood as a grim testament to the erosion of press freedom. India, which ranked 161 out of 180 countries in Reporters Without Borders' World Press Freedom Index 2023, witnessed a series of severe crackdowns on dissenting voices.[80]

The release of a two-part BBC documentary titled *India: The Modi Question* was a significant event in this crackdown. This documentary critically examined PM Modi's involvement in the 2002 Gujarat violence and scrutinized his government's treatment of Muslims since 2014. The government's response was swift and severe; the documentary was blocked, and tax department officials raided BBC offices in India on the pretext of an income tax survey.[81]

---

[78] Ibid.
[79] Ibid.
[80] Ibid.
[81] Ellis-Petersen, Hannah, and Jim Waterson, 'BBC offices in India raided by tax officials amid Modi documentary fallout', *The Guardian*, 14 February 2023, https://tinyurl.com/bde9e2b7. Accessed on 11 November 2024.

In the wake of these events, early morning police raids were carried out on the offices of *NewsClick*, an independent news portal known for its critical stance. The Delhi Police arrested its founder Prabir Purkayastha under the stringent UAPA, casting a chilling shadow over the journalistic community.[82] In another striking instance, journalist Siddique Kappan was arrested while on his way to cover the Hathras gangrape case involving a Dalit girl.[83] His detention underscored the perils faced by those who sought to report on issues questioning the Modi government. Nearly 50 journalists, activists and comedians across India found their homes invaded by the police invoking anti-terrorism laws. Among those caught in the sweep were journalist Paranjoy Guha Thakurta, renowned for his investigative work,[84] activist Teesta Setalvad, a stalwart defender of human rights,[85] and comedian Sanjay Rajoura, whose biting satire often targeted the establishment.[86] Each faced intense police questioning, their lives upended by the sudden and brutal enforcement actions.

New laws targeted independent digital media, including many critical journalists who had moved online, like Ravish Kumar, whose YouTube channel amassed 1.13 crore subscribers. In April,

---

[82] Vishwanath, Apurva, 'In NewsClick founder Prabir Purkayastha's release, how arrest protection was extended to stringent UAPA provisions', *The Indian Express*, 17 May 2024, https://tinyurl.com/mvx9kbsb. Accessed on 23 December 2024.

[83] 'Kerala journalist on his way to Hathras detained by UP police, journalist union files petition in Supreme Court', *Newslaundry*, 6 October 2020, https://tinyurl.com/Kerala-journalist-Hathras. Accessed on 14 January 2025.

[84] Zafar, Hanan, and Jyoti Thakur, 'How the Indian government is weaponizing laws to silence and intimidate journalists', *IJNET*, 14 May 2024, https://tinyurl.com/journalist-intimidation. Accessed on 14 January 2025.

[85] 'Raid on NewsClick: Mumbai Police conducts searches at activist Teesta Stelvad's Juhu residence', *The Times of India*, 3 October 2023, https://tinyurl.com/rh8dysbr. Accessed on 14 January 2025.

[86] Mateen, Zoya, 'NewsClick: India police arrest journalists over China funding claims', *BBC*, 3 October 2023, https://tinyurl.com/3yksbdmk. Accessed on 14 January 2025.

independent YouTube channels such as *Bolta Hindustan* and *National Dastak* were blocked under directives from the Ministry of Information and Broadcasting.[87] Videos by digital journalists Meghnad and Sohit Mishra questioning the integrity of electronic voting machines were also restricted.[88] Yet, Abhinandan Sekhri, the chief executive of *Newslaundry*, observed that independent media was gaining more visibility despite government pushback. He believed the public was growing weary of the hatred towards television media and increasingly supported independent digital media outlets.[89]

As public life turned into a divided house, film producers took to carefully scripted propaganda movies to spread fake impressions against Congress. Films like *The Kashmir Files*, *The Kerala Story* and *The Vaccine War* emerged, further polarizing an already fragmented society.

As these events unfolded, international watchdogs and human rights organizations sounded the alarm, condemning the government's actions and highlighting the perilous state of press freedom in the country.[90] [91] Despite the adversity, a chorus of voices within India and beyond rose in defence of free speech, challenging the oppressive measures and striving to uphold democratic principles in the face of mounting authoritarianism.

---

[87]Dutta, Anisha, 'Small signs of hope—but a long way to go—for Indian media independence', *Columbia Journalism Review*, https://tinyurl.com/2vkjaayp. Accessed on 11 November 2024.
[88]Ibid.
[89]Ibid.
[90]'Watchdog: India has failed to protect journalists', *Al Jazeera*, 29 August 2016, https://tinyurl.com/India-journalists. Accessed on 14 January 2025.
[91]'India's press freedom has rapidly declined in recent years: Data', *The Hindu*, 15 May 2024, https://tinyurl.com/India-press-freedom. Accessed on 14 January 2025.

TWO

BHARAT JODO YATRA: THE VOICE OF BHARAT MATA

For some observers, the crisis in the Congress party was an existential one. Attrition continued to bleed our party. Important leaders, many of whom had received attention at the highest quarters of the party, left for the BJP. The Congress would not and could not subscribe to this crisis and mentally returned to the drawing board to plan a revival in somewhat existential circumstances. A quick look at the timeline of the Congress party's endeavour to recapture lost ground and the imagination of the voter will clarify the journey to 99 seats for the Congress and 232 for the INDIA Alliance in 2024.

The usual toning up and reorganizational steps were underway to overhaul the party. At one point, election wizard Prashant Kishor was brought in to inject new energy into Uttar Pradesh ahead of the 2017 assembly polls, with campaigns like *khaat sabhas* (charpoy meetings). In due course, Kishor briefly offered to join the Congress party as an activist with the special responsibility of a vice president for elections. Not being encouraged beyond a few presentations, he chose to float his own political outfit in Bihar.

The Chintan Shivir, held at Udaipur from 13 to 15 May 2022, marked a pivotal moment for the Congress party as it sought to recover from prolonged and repeated electoral defeats. The gathering aimed to reenergize the party and strategize for the future. The most salient message came from Congress President Sonia Gandhi, who declared, *Karz chukane ka samay aa gaya hai* (It's time to repay Congress party's debt)—a call to repay the debt to the party's legacy and supporters.[1] This statement set the tone for the Shivir, reflecting the urgency and seriousness with which the Congress approached the challenges ahead.

In his valedictory address at the Nav Sankalp Chintan Shivir

---

[1] '"Congress gave us everything, now time to repay debts": Sonia Gandhi at Chintan Shivir', *News 18*, 13 May 2022, https://tinyurl.com/yfyyfm6b. Accessed on 12 November 2024.

in Udaipur on 15 May, Rahul Gandhi signalled a significant shift in the party's approach, emphasizing the need to 'transform the nature of the Congress party'.[2] He clarified that this transformation was not about changing the party's ideology or core beliefs but about revolutionizing the way the Congress functioned.

The first step in this direction was the 'to-do list' approved by the Congress Working Committee (CWC), the party's highest decision-making body. It outlined a detailed strategy for how the party intended to operate in the future. The CWC focused on two key issues—strengthening the organization and becoming battle-ready for the upcoming elections. One of the crucial proposals greenlighted by the CWC was the formation of a Political Affairs Committee—a sub-group of the CWC tasked with implementing the programme and providing strategic advice. Public affairs committees were also established in the party's state units to ensure alignment and coordination at all levels.

In his speech, Rahul emphasized running the organization more scientifically and professionally. He insisted that decisions be based on proper scientific feedback, moving away from ad-hoc methods and ensuring that the party's actions were data-driven and strategically sound.

Rahul also underscored the importance of a mass contact programme. He emphasized that there were 'no shortcuts' and urged all members, regardless of age or position, to directly engage with the people of India. He stressed the need to understand people's aspirations and effectively communicate the Congress's achievements and its future intentions.

Rahul acknowledged that the twenty-first century was fundamentally about communication and admitted that Congress

---

[2]Indian National Congress, 'Shri Rahul Gandhi addressed the closing ceremony of Nav Sankalp Shivir, Udaipur', https://tinyurl.com/bdd3x5a6. Accessed on 12 November 2024.

had been outperformed by its opponents. 'They have much more money than us and they are better at communication than we are,' he observed.[3] Recognizing this gap, he called for a complete overhaul of the party's communications system, emphasizing the need to connect with the people of India, particularly the youth, in a new and dynamic way.

The resolution for this new approach was prepared overnight by Varun Santosh and Pawan Khera and later edited by Randeep Singh Surjewala, the then general secretary and in-charge of AICC's Communications Department, along with Abhay Dubey. Political activist Yogendra Yadav had discussed the idea of a call to action with Surjewala and Santosh. Khera proposed that the call to action should be *Bharat Jodo*. While reinforcing the need for a strong call to action, Jairam Ramesh, General Secretary In-charge Communications, insisted that Bharat Jodo be repeated three times for emphasis.

The Pied Piper Leads People

As part of this renewed effort, Rahul Gandhi committed to leading Congress from the front in the run-up to the 2024 Lok Sabha elections. This commitment began with the unprecedented Bharat Jodo Yatra, a mass outreach programme. Starting from Kanyakumari at the southernmost tip of the subcontinent on 7 September 2022 and extending to the valley of Jammu and Kashmir, the yatra symbolized the party's resolve to reconnect with the grassroots and unify the nation under its banner.

The resolution marked the beginning of a new chapter for Congress, a moment where the party set out to rebuild itself by learning from past mistakes, embracing modern strategies, and reconnecting with the people. Despite the many hurdles

---
[3] Ibid.

created by the BJP, including the freezing of party bank accounts and ED raids on Opposition leaders, the Congress persisted.[4] These challenges, designed to weaken the party, did not stop its momentum. In fact, Congress managed to improve its tally in the following elections, proving its resilience and adaptability.

There was also widespread concern among party cadres about the political landscape. While some steadfastly repudiated the Hindutva clarion calls, they refrained from questioning the broader claim for the Ram Mandir, rejecting any attempt to inject divisive politics into the issue. The party's position, however, received a notable boost with the appointment of an experienced Dalit president, Mallikarjun Kharge, after Sonia Gandhi dismissed pleas for another term. Kharge's election as president, defeating Shashi Tharoor, strengthened the party's resolve.

Throughout the Bharat Jodo Yatra, Rahul prioritized connecting with the Dalit communities in every district he passed through. His unwavering commitment to engaging with these groups gradually strengthened his credibility among Dalit intellectuals. As his outreach deepened, so did his influence. Over time, his framing of the BJP's attacks on the Constitution as direct assaults on Dr B.R. Ambedkar and the Dalit community began to resonate more powerfully within these circles. His message gained traction, marking a significant shift in how these critical issues were perceived and discussed. What appeared at first blush to be an implausible, challenging plan metamorphosed into a massive people's movement, merging Congress workers with ordinary citizens who enthusiastically came out in support.

Apart from common citizens and Congress party workers, the march saw a glittering presence of actors such as Urmila

---

[4]'23 of 25 Opposition leaders accused of corruption got reprieve after joining BJP since 2014: Report', *Mint*, 3 April 2024, https://tinyurl.com/BJP-corruption. Accessed on 14 January 2025.

Matondkar, Swara Bhaskar, Pooja Bhatt and Riya Sen, activists Anand Patwardhan, Aruna Roy and Radhika Vemula, musician T.M. Krishna, comedian Kunal Kamra and former Reserve Bank of India governor, Raghuram Rajan.

With each step, Rahul grew in stature and found a place in the hearts of children, women and men of all ages. He paused in places to talk to opinion makers, interest groups like farmers and workers, professionals, sportspersons, think tanks—virtual pied piper-led trains of people searching for something novel and meaningful to overcome the ennui of contemporary politics. However, when asked if the Bharat Jodo Yatra had successfully bolstered his image, Rahul stunned his audience by saying, 'Rahul Gandhi is just your imagination; I have killed him!'[5]

The icing on the cake came when the Yatra reached the Kashmir valley on 27 January 2023 and made its way to Srinagar through streets lined with locals braving snowfall and freezing temperatures. In the first major political activity in the region since the abrogation of Article 370 in 2019, huge crowds turned up to welcome Rahul for the end of his march.

Rahul spoke of coming back home and touched hearts as he recalled the sad moments when the phone rang in a faraway place in India to deliver the news of his grandmother's death and a few years later, of his father's assassination. 'I pray that you good people never have to get such calls ever,' he said to the gathered crowd. In a moment, years of pain and anger disappeared. Quite separate from the government's professed commitment to bring normalcy in Jammu and Kashmir, Rahul Gandhi had triggered a palpable change.

The Bharat Jodo Yatra had not only galvanized common people

---

[5] '"Rahul Gandhi is just your imagination, I have killed him…" Congress leader on his public image', *ANI News*, 9 January 2023, https://tinyurl.com/ype8vb7x. Accessed on 12 November 2024.

across all sectors and regions but was also closely watched by all political parties. Welcoming Rahul, who highlighted his Kashmiri 'roots', Dr Farooq Abdullah, former chief minister of Jammu and Kashmir, travelled 350 kilometres from Srinagar to Lakhanpur in Jammu. Abdullah compared Rahul's journey from Kanyakumari to Kashmir with the one that Vedic scholar Adi Shankaracharya undertook in the eighth century. Omar Abdullah, who had served as chief minister of Jammu and Kashmir from 2009 to 2015 and began his second term as CM in 2024, marched alongside Rahul in Banihal in Ramban district. Rahul was joined by another former chief minister, Mehbooba Mufti, along with her daughter, Iltija Mufti, in Chersoo village in Awantipora. Priyanka Gandhi Vadra, Congress General Secretary, also joined her brother on the final leg of the yatra in Kashmir.

The Bharat Jodo Yatra culminated in a rally at a stadium in Srinagar on 30 January, coinciding with Mahatma Gandhi's death anniversary. The event saw leaders from political parties from across the country share the stage for the first time, including members of the Dravida Munnetra Kazhagam (DMK), the National Conference (NC), the People's Democratic Party (PDP), the Communist Party of India (CPI), the Revolutionary Socialist Party (RSP), and the Indian Union Muslim League (IUML).

Addressing the rally, Rahul said he was warned against travelling on foot by the local administration, who said a grenade might be hurled at him.[6] But he insisted on walking because his 'family and [Mahatma] Gandhi taught me to live fearlessly, otherwise, that is not living.'[7]

---

[6]"Bharat Jodo Yatra Highlights: Was warned I might be attacked in Kashmir, but people here gave me love, not hand grenades, says Rahul Gandhi", *The Indian Express*, 30 January 2023, https://tinyurl.com/4jhz9aak. Accessed on 23 December 2024.
[7]"Bharat Jodo Yatra: Rahul Gandhi's unity march ends in Kashmir", *BBC*, 30 January 2023, https://tinyurl.com/ypvdetj2. Accessed on 12 November 2024.

Assembly Elections: Expect the Unexpected

A lot was turning positive for the Congress, including victory in the Karnataka assembly elections in May—we won 135 seats in the 224-member Legislative Assembly, while the BJP and the JD(S) settled for 66 and 19 seats, respectively.[8] We overcame intense competition between claimants for the chief minister's post to settle for Siddaramaiah, with D.K. Shivakumar as his deputy.

Karnataka was the first step on the long road to recovery. A few months later, the assembly elections in five states of Telangana, Madhya Pradesh, Rajasthan, Chhattisgarh and Mizoram were expected to be a solid reply to the BJP. But sadly, except for Telangana, an important saving grace, we did not achieve our objective.

Telangana saw the Congress secure 64 seats while the BJP managed just eight, with the Bharat Rashtra Samithi (BRS) winning 39 seats and the All India Majlis-e-Ittehadul Muslimeen (AIMIM) capturing seven.[9] In Madhya Pradesh, Congress won 66 seats against the BJP's dominant 163.[10] Meanwhile, Rajasthan's elections resulted in 69 seats for the Congress and 115 for the BJP.[11] In Chhattisgarh, the Congress won 35 seats, whereas the BJP garnered 54.[12]

---

[8] 'General Election To Vidhan Sabha Trends & Result May-2023-Karnataka', Election Commission of India, https://tinyurl.com/2s46fzeh. Accessed on 3 December 2024.

[9] General Election to Assembly Constituencies: Trends & Results Dec-2023-Telangana, Election Commission of India, https://tinyurl.com/26esvzka. Accessed on 3 December 2024.

[10] General Election to Assembly Constituencies: Trends & Results Dec-2023-Madhya Pradesh, Election Commission of India, https://tinyurl.com/43x8r9u7. Accessed on 3 December 2024.

[11] General Election to Assembly Constituencies: Trends & Results Dec-2023-Rajasthan, Election Commission of India, https://tinyurl.com/2nfskync. Accessed on 3 December 2024.

[12] General Election to Assembly Constituencies: Trends & Results Dec-2023-Chhattisgarh, Election Commission of India, https://tinyurl.com/27kysrdf. Accessed on 3 December 2024.

These results were definitely not what we had expected. However, the same cannot be said about the common talk in political circles—that discontent within the BJP had been simmering. Shivraj Singh Chouhan, who had served as the chief minister of Madhya Pradesh for over 16 years, and Vasundhara Raje, a two-term chief minister of Rajasthan, found themselves sidelined in a party that once relied heavily on their leadership. The BJP's decision to elevate fresh and younger faces to lead the governments in Madhya Pradesh and Rajasthan left the political future of these two former chief ministers hanging in uncertainty, and left them smarting for being deprived of their rightful opportunities.

Both Chouhan and Raje had been handpicked by the Atal Bihari Vajpayee and L.K. Advani leadership, and over the years, they transformed themselves into powerful regional satraps in their respective states. For Raje, the sting of this sidelining was particularly sharp. As the daughter of Vijaya Raje Scindia, one of the founding figures of the erstwhile Jan Sangh, she carried a legacy deeply intertwined with the party's history. However, when the BJP returned to power in Rajasthan, the signals from the central leadership were unmistakable. Vasundhara Raje was not only passed over for the CM's chair despite her seniority, but was also handed the humiliating task of announcing the name of Bhajan Lal Sharma, a first-time MLA, as the new chief minister. The name was written on a note delivered by Rajnath Singh from New Delhi, leaving no room for discussion or dissent. Sharma's ascension as the 'chit-wala CM' of Rajasthan happened right under Raje's nose, a clear indication that the party's central leadership no longer had confidence in her.[13]

A report by *The Caravan* pointed out that on 20 October

---

[13]Bhandari, Prakash, and Vasundhara Raje, 'The wounded tigress', *National Herald*, 12 June 2024, https://tinyurl.com/yudz2fpt. Accessed on 3 December 2024.

2024, the BJP issued an extraordinary appeal by PM Modi to the voters in Madhya Pradesh.[14] The appeal urged them to ensure a BJP victory in the upcoming state elections on 17 November by directly supporting Modi. The appeal prominently featured a picture of Modi at the top, with four-term chief minister Shivraj Singh Chouhan receiving only a brief, one-line mention in the text, acknowledging his role in spearheading the party's work in the state. Another photograph underscored Modi's dominance, foregrounding him at the bottom, while Chouhan and several other BJP leaders, including many from Madhya Pradesh, were relegated to the background.[15]

In the days leading up to the appeal's release, Chouhan had turned to his constituents with a sense of desperation, seeking reassurance from the people who had once embraced him as their leader. 'I want to ask you whether I am running a good government or a bad government. So, should this government move ahead or not? Should *Mama* (affectionate term by which he was known in Madhya Pradesh) become chief minister or not?' he pleaded, his voice betraying the unease that had settled in his heart.[16]

The BJP's central leadership, under PM Modi's influence, began to shift its focus away from regional leaders like Chouhan, instead promoting PM Modi as the sole face of the party's success. This shift was painfully evident in the appeal released on 20 October, where Chouhan's contributions were reduced to a mere footnote in a narrative dominated by Modi's image and name.

The discontent within Chouhan was palpable. He had long prided himself on his connection with the people of Madhya Pradesh, who affectionately referred to him as 'Mama'. Yet now,

---

[14]Singh Bal, Hartosh, 'Cutting Mama down to size', *The Caravan*, 15 November 2023, https://tinyurl.com/mvna7r7n. Accessed on 3 December 2024.
[15]Ibid.
[16]Ibid.

he faced the reality that his role within the party was diminishing, his identity as a leader subsumed under PM Modi's towering persona. The appeal was not just a call for votes but also a stark reminder that the BJP, under PM Modi's leadership, was moving in a direction where regional leaders like Chouhan were becoming increasingly irrelevant.

As Chouhan grappled with this new reality, the tension between him and PM Modi grew more pronounced. The camaraderie they had once shared, built on their parallel political paths, was now strained by the centralization of power in the hands of PM Modi. Chouhan's appeal to his constituents, asking if he should continue as CM, reflected a deep-seated anxiety—a recognition that his political future was no longer secure and that his position within the party was no longer guaranteed. This was a bitter pill to swallow for a leader who had once been the face of the BJP in Madhya Pradesh.

Nitin Gadkari openly opposed his re-election bid, along with further reports of growing differences with Yogi Adityanath, particularly regarding Arvind Kumar Sharma, a former Gujarat-cadre bureaucrat brought to Uttar Pradesh and appointed as BJP state vice-president. Then, there was a perception that the RSS cadre avoided active participation. This was underscored by the statement of BJP president J.P. Nadda in response to a question on how the RSS presence had changed since the time of PM Vajpayee, in which he noted, '*Shuru mein hum aksham honge, thora kum honge, RSS ki zaroorat padti thi… Aaj hum badh gaye hain, saksham hai…toh BJP apne aap ko chalati hai* (In the beginning, we would have been less capable, smaller, and needed the RSS. Today, we have grown, and we are capable. The BJP runs itself).[17]

---

[17] Mathew, Liz, 'Nadda on BJP-RSS ties: We have grown, more capable now… the BJP runs itself', *The Indian Express*, 2 May 2024, https://tinyurl.com/bdmcx5ej. Accessed on 3 December 2024.

The discontent simmered beneath the surface, reflecting the broader challenges facing regional leaders in a party increasingly dominated by PM Modi's image and influence.

Uniting India through Justice

This influence had little impact on the Bharat Jodo Yatra, which began with the aim of connecting directly with the people of India through traditional methods, as the BJP largely monopolized modern communication tools. During this first yatra, Rahul gained an insight into the values and aspirations of the people by listening to hundreds and thousands of voices from India.

The second—the Bharat Jodo Nyay Yatra, proposed at the CWC meeting just a few months before the 2024 elections—was designed to steer the people's voice towards promoting a vision for India with composite culture, harmony and tolerance as its concrete social basis, and a democratic, production led-economy, which was embodied in the NYAY Patra, the Congress's comprehensive manifesto for the 2024 Lok Sabha elections.[18]

The Nyay Yatra began in Manipur on 14 January 2024, following Rahul's visit to the riot-hit state. It was a visit that underscored his commitment to his ideal of *Mohabbat ki dukan* (shop of love). Rahul sought to establish a direct connection with the people during his campaign. Initially, a truck had been designed for his travel, but he soon felt this creating a physical and emotional distance between him and the crowds. Feeling too far from those he wanted to engage with, he decided to switch to a car, allowing him to be closer to people and interact with them more personally. This change reflected his desire for a more intimate and authentic connection with the public.

---

[18] 'Nyay Patra – Lok Sabha Elections 2024', Indian National Congress, https://tinyurl.com/c3d395xa. Accessed on 12 November 2024.

Throughout the yatra, Rahul's daily activities and speeches resonated with three key themes—hope (*asha*), trust (*vishwas*), and companionship (*humsafar*). Various stakeholders were involved in designing and executing his interactions with civil society members, intellectuals and victims of atrocities.

A distinctive feature of Rahul's approach was his ability to humanize data. His communications team, led by Y.B. Srivatsa and colleagues, including Smit Singh, focused on transforming his ideas and insights into detailed, actionable plans. They aimed to convey complex economic and social vision through ordinary ideas such as caste and economic census. In his speech in Bokaro in February, he bridged social and economic questions, merging them together in simple language into a unified force for change. The message of *mohabbat* (love) was consistently linked to key issues such as education, employment, healthcare and social security.

Similarly, data on atrocities was brought to life through the experiences of victims in Manipur, while data on hate crimes was framed through historical references such as Nathuram Godse, connecting these incidents to a broader discourse on the idea of India. Rahul's message was easily conveyed—his idea of India is to love and treasure diversity and justice, while that of the Rashtriya Swayamsevak Sangh (RSS) is to hate, divide, and create space for injustice against the unprivileged. For Rahul, the first condition of being an Indian is to love, while the first condition of being a follower of Godse is to hate.

These campaigns, fuelled by Rahul's visionary leadership, were anchored in the principles of love, justice and equality, demonstrating the Congress's determination to rebuild and adapt to contemporary challenges. Both yatras revitalized the Congress cadre, imbuing them with renewed energy and purpose while inspiring hope among countless individuals outside the party who shared the vision of an inclusive and united India. They became a powerful reminder of the 'Idea of India', resonating deeply with citizens who yearned to return to the values of harmony and justice.

The yatra had redefined the nation's political discourse in the lead-up to the Lok Sabha elections by focusing on the aspirations of India's diverse population. By championing the values of democracy, justice and diversity, Congress presented a compelling vision for the nation's future—one of inclusion and empowerment. This approach positioned the Congress not merely as a political force but also as a beacon of hope for an India where every voice was valued, and every citizen was empowered. The campaign left an indelible mark on the electorate, reshaping perceptions and reaffirming the party's relevance in the evolving political landscape.

Rahul's commitment to this journey extended beyond the elections. He continued his yatra, meeting everyday Indians whose contributions built the country—carpenters, bike mechanics, barbers, shoemakers and countless others. This evolved form of the yatra embodied a deeper connection with the people, reflecting a relentless pursuit of a better, more inclusive India. The journey was no longer just about political resurgence but about reaffirming the ideals that unite the nation and bridging the gaps that divide it. In this renewed form, the yatra became a symbol of hope, endurance, and the shared dream for a brighter future.

THREE

INDIA: UNITING TO DEFEND THE IDEA OF INDIA

Several leaders from different parties had spoken of the need to come together to oust the BJP government, despite—or perhaps because of—their sustained efforts to capture the psyche of the Indian voter permanently. PM Modi, the 56-inch-chest protagonist, the champion of Balakot, a spotless hero who unselfconsciously brushed off the fatalities on the Line of Actual Control (LAC), who claimed to pause the Russia-Ukraine war,[1] who captured the hearts of Muslim women by criminalizing Triple Talaq, ruthlessly contained the CAA protests, abrogated Article 370, left no stone unturned to rapidly build the Ram Temple in Ayodhya, and announced the arrival of the Uniform Civil Code (UCC) and One Country One Election. Even without a somewhat pliant ECI, he had gathered enough material to believe he was seriously en route to '400 paar'. For his opponents, it was feared to be an election to end all elections.

The ground statistics remained uninfluenced by the divisive rhetoric and tall performance claims. The leader of the world's third-largest economy and the G20 was poised to return to power unless the Opposition came together and claimed their collective share of the election pie. The sad truth about India's accelerated growth was the use of hoardings and screens to hide the shanties and open drains of urban India. The Swachh Bharat Mission had come to naught with garbage spread across the landscape and piled into virtual hillocks.

There was much speculation about whether a full-scale nationwide alliance that would move mountains was possible. About then, I was asked to attend the eleventh All India Party Congress of the Communist Party of India (Marxist-Leninist) Liberation [CPI(ML)] in Patna in February 2023.

---

[1] Singh, Kanwardeep, 'PM Narendra Modi government got Russia-Ukraine war stopped to rescue Indians', *The Times of India*, 2 May 2024, https://tinyurl.com/3fzcrb8r. Accessed on 14 January 2025.

The allies, Janata Dal-United (JDU) and Rashtriya Janata Dal (RJD), were naturally represented by Nitish Kumar, Chief Minister of Bihar, and Tejashwi Yadav, Deputy Chief Minister, respectively. When Nitish spoke, he alluded to procrastination of the alliance decision spread over several months. When I got a chance to speak, to lighten the mood, I retorted, 'Nitishji, when you fall in love, it takes a while to say I love you.' Indeed, it is often a matter of who says it first. This caught the imagination of the audience, and they burst out laughing.

Subsequently, Bihar leaders were invited to Delhi to meet Kharge and Rahul. I was lucky to be included in the Congress delegation. The conversation was a bit frosty to begin with. Nitish underscored that crucial time had been lost in the three months since the matter was first broached. Yet, there was a studied silence. He suddenly changed track and asked if he should 'touch the feet of our leaders' to persuade them to take the step that would inevitably benefit them rather than any other person. And then everything changed. Rahul spoke of the need to meet at length, perhaps for several days, to work out the contours of the alliance. But Nitish was a man in a hurry. He offered to speak to Mamata Banerjee, Akhilesh Yadav and even Arvind Kejriwal, leaving Sharad Pawar and DMK to the Congress. His statement got him a *carte blanche*, including the Aam Aadmi Party (AAP). It looked as though we were in business. Events moved so fast that the usual insiders were left to send text messages quizzing about the details.

Nitish acted swiftly, reaching out to Kejriwal within a few hours. What had seemed impossible because of the ongoing antagonism between Congress and AAP workers was quickly accomplished. Responses from other potential partners also came forward, but it was not easy to move forward to formal meetings. The logistics of securing the alliance's structure was left to the

Congress for practical reasons, but this meant there was no firm decision on a secretariat for the alliance or combined committees for logistics and media. Under the leadership of Jairam Ramesh, the Congress Communications Department assumed control and engaged effectively with the leaders of the INDIA bloc through ad hoc outreach efforts. Inevitably, there were minor hiccups from time to time and one-upmanship in scheduling of joint public meetings beyond the three informal gatherings of party leaders before these joint public meetings.

Finding Common Ground amid Divisions

Understandably, there were imponderables to be handled in the nascent alliance. There was speculation about who would lead the alliance. A consensus emerged that we would pursue collective leadership, and the leaders would decide together on the leadership issue after the elections. However, Stalin of the DMK publicly came out in support of Rahul. Whatever the views of each leader may have been, it was clear that the Congress leadership was at the top, and most people understood that the party would get the largest number of seats. Yet, the leadership issue was strategically kept on the back burner. As it turned out in Parliament, the largest alliance party would take the lead, and the LOP's position would inevitably descend upon the Congress.

Nitish seemed anxious about being appointed convener of the alliance, but there was a lack of clarity for several reasons. Mamata had reservations about the Left, and the RJD had its worries. The matter could not be settled at several party leaders' meetings, leading to visible tension. It reached a point where Nitish disassociated himself from the issue of becoming a convener. Something snapped, and suddenly he chose to rejoin the BJP in Bihar and abandon the INDIA Alliance project. Although he could have been motivated by the seeming delay in appointment as convener, the actual calculation might have been the struggle of the JDU and RJD cadres. The RJD also sought to speak for their partner during the seat negotiations.

The team to negotiate the seat arrangement was headed by Rajya Sabha MP Mukul Wasnik, and included me, Mohan Prakash, Ashok Gehlot and Bhupesh Baghel. Wasnik has an impressive record of long years of service as General Secretary in most states and brought invaluable information to the table. The last two had other important issues to attend to and were able to give little time to the negotiations.

The matter left to the three of us was handled in earnest over two months, from February to April 2024. We spent many hours trying to find common ground with the AAP, which wanted to get a large share of the seven seats in Delhi, Chandigarh and Bharuch in Gujarat. Chandigarh had been Pawan Bansal's seat, and Bharuch was late Ahmed Patel's home territory. These were the most difficult seats for us to give up, but the AAP was adamant, which was somewhat insensitive considering that the Patel siblings were anxious to retain Bharuch, to the point of virtual breakdown. In Punjab, both sides thought it wise to fight independently and not cede opposition space to the BJP. The inherent difficulty of uniting after intense rivalry and competition for the space made it challenging to bring workers in favour of our decision. However, after deciding to push the alliance, Congress leadership showed maximum restraint and accommodation. For the Congress worker, we accomplished the impossible. However, the synergy we had hoped for did not develop during the campaign, and sadly, today we have little to show for our efforts in terms of the Delhi results.

Relatively speaking, the negotiations in Bihar, Jharkhand, Maharashtra and Tamil Nadu went smoothly, though not without sporadic difficulties. While Sharad Pawar steered the Maharashtra partners deftly, the Shiv Sena were demanding but reasonable bargainers. The two partners NCP and Shiv Sena were both numerically disadvantaged because of a split in their elected members but had great sympathy for the ordinary people. The main issue was whether the seats would be considered even if the incumbent had changed due to the split. We lost our negotiating leader, Ashok Chavan, midway when he left to join the BJP in February. Yet the final tally from Maharashtra was very encouraging.

What initially appeared a challenging task turned out to be the best arrangement, followed by a nearly 100 per cent result in Tamil Nadu. In keeping with tradition, Wasnik led our team to Chennai for the first round of talks, followed by other rounds in New Delhi. Minor hesitations were addressed when the Congress President and Rahul spoke to Stalin, clearing the mist.

The longest negotiations took place with the Samajwadi Party (SP) in my home state of Uttar Pradesh. As days went by, there was no sign of movement. So I took the initiative to speak to Ram Gopal Yadav, Secretary General of the Samajwadi Party, who was most reassuring and said we could seal the arrangement in a few sittings. I messaged national president of the party Akhilesh Yadav, who called me back to say I should have a word with Abu Asim Azmi, the chief of Samajwadi Party's Maharashtra unit, in Mumbai, and a list of the negotiating team would be sent soon.

We received the list from Ram Gopal Yadav, Javed Ali Khan, Udaiveer Singh, Lalji Verma and Sangram Singh Yadav, and devised a method to get a fix on the negotiation landscape. We tried to steer them away from the 2019 Lok Sabha election results and focus on the 2009 election results instead. In that election, we won 21 seats, gaining 12 from 2004, while they lost 12 and secured 23 seats.[2] However, our talks on seat sharing had broken

---

[2] Party-wise Seats Won and Votes Polled (%), Lok Sabha 2009.

down. This tough call was up to Sonia Gandhi alone. Of course, since then we have lost candidates like Annu Tandon to them and others to the BJP (Jitin Prasada and R.P.N. Singh).

Ajay Rai, President of the Uttar Pradesh Congress Committee (UPCC), wanted to fight 40 seats, something we all felt was a bit ambitious and exaggerated, but looking back, one can admit that his expectation was not misplaced. Even as we talked, the Samajwadi Party started to issue lists of the seats they wanted to leave to us and those for which they were fielding their candidates. The Samajwadi Party started with eleven seats for the Congress and finally reached seventeen. At one stage, as negotiations got bogged down, General Secretary Avinash Pandey took charge of the Uttar Pradesh Congress. But, in effect, he took instructions from Priyanka Gandhi, who had worked very hard in the state for the 2019 assembly elections and knew the ground very closely. She was anxious to seal the deal to utilize the few remaining days of the Bharat Jodo Nyay Yatra to show joint solidarity with the Samajwadi Party. The yatra reached Kanpur in February 2024, where Akhilesh joined, and that became the hallmark of joint appearances at several campaign meetings.

To tell the truth, the negotiations were surreal. We were not very certain about our strengths, though there was enough information that the Muslims were returning to the Congress in a big way, even ahead of the Samajwadi Party and the BSP. Yet, it seemed too early to build an electoral strategy around Muslims. Samajwadi Party leaders were pressing for an alliance with the Congress to avoid a BSP-like decline. Despite the party's top leadership refusing to acknowledge the resurgence of Congress publicly, they joined the INDIA Alliance. They opted to combine non-Yadav backwards, taking Yadavs' support for granted. Communities like Nishad, Shakya, Rajbhar, Kurmi, Lodhi, et al., were accommodated, and only five Yadavs—all from Mulayam Singh's family—were given tickets. It certainly paid off for the Samajwadi Party, but it remains to be seen how stable this arrangement will be.

When it came to my constituency of Farrukhabad, I had stepped away from the discussions as a matter of propriety. This amused my colleagues but allowed the Samajwadi Party to announce its candidate for the seat my family and I had held for decades but with breaks. For all of us, it was imperative to clinch the deal with the Samajwadi Party for the alliance's credibility, particularly in North India. The greater cause prevailed with all of us, ignoring personal disappointments. I felt my obligation was to get success on pan-India seats rather than worry about my career. That meant that I had to sit out the election; despite highly respected religious leaders like Maulana Arshad Madani, President of the Jamiat Ulama-e-Hind, and Maulana Khalid Rasheed of Ulama-e-Farangi Mahal trying to persuade the Samajwadi Party leadership, it refused to budge on Farrukhabad. Various explanations were offered for this intransigence, including the fact that Congress had not sought the seat.

Learning to converse with open hearts and making acknowledged accommodations would have been more rewarding. This would indeed have laid a stronger foundation for future cooperation and trust. At the risk of sounding self-centred, it must be frankly said that in twenty years, there has not been the Muslim support for the Congress we saw this time. Obviously, where there was a non-Congress alliance candidate, he got Muslim votes in abundance. How relevant will that be for future planning? That is anyone's guess. The Farrukhabad seat was sadly lost to the BJP, with the incumbent Member of Parliament, Mukesh Rajput, getting a third term.

During the negotiations, Pallavi Patel, leader of the Apna Dal (Kamerawadi), left the INDIA Alliance (read SP) after its demand for Mirzapur, Phulpur and Kaushambi Lok Sabha seats was unmet. The Apna Dal (K) made a strategic move by allying with the All India Majlis-e-Ittehadul Muslimeen (AIMIM), branding it as PDM (Pichda, Dalit, Muslim) Nyay Morcha. This alliance aimed at consolidating support among marginalized communities, presenting a direct challenge to Akhilesh's PDA (Pichda, Dalit, Alpsankhyak).

In the early stages of the seat-sharing discussions, the Samajwadi Party had initially listed Surendra Singh Patel as the candidate for the Varanasi seat on its third list. Patel, a seasoned politician, had previously served as a Member of Legislative Council (MLC) for Sevapuri assembly seat between 2012 and 2017, and held the influential positions of Minister of State for Public Works Department and Irrigation during Akhilesh's tenure as chief minister. Simultaneously, Ajay Rai, a prominent political figure with five terms as MLA under his belt and serving as the UPCC president, was setting his sights on the Ballia seat. The demographics of Ballia, with 20 per cent Brahmins and eight per cent Bhumihars, seemed to favour Rai, who belonged to the Bhumihar community. He believed that the caste dynamics were aligned in his favour, giving him a solid chance at victory. However, the Samajwadi Party, holding three of the five sitting MLAs in the Ballia Lok Sabha constituency, was unwilling to relinquish this crucial seat to the Congress. They remained resolute, refusing to engage in negotiations that would see the seat go to the Congress, effectively shutting down Rai's ambitions for Ballia.

As the negotiations continued, the strategic significance of the Varanasi seat, especially given its association with PM Modi, became increasingly apparent. Both parties recognized that Varanasi, with its symbolic importance at the national level, required a tactful approach. The Samajwadi Party leadership, upon further reflection, realized that fielding their candidate, particularly someone from the OBC community, might inadvertently polarize the electorate.

Such polarization could alienate other caste groups, leading to a fragmented vote, ultimately weakening their prospects in this critical constituency.

This insight led to a pivotal moment in the discussions. The Samajwadi Party, after careful consideration of the potential ramifications, decided to cede the Varanasi seat to the Congress. This decision was rooted in the belief that Rai, with his extensive political experience and strong local ties, had a better chance of uniting the diverse voter base under the Congress banner. With the Samajwadi Party stepping aside, Rai was officially declared the Congress candidate for Varanasi.

This decision marked a significant shift in the region's electoral landscape. It was a move that set the stage for a fiercely contested battle, one that even caused concern within the ranks of the ruling BJP.

In the end, despite the challenges and initial hurdles, the INDIA Alliance showcased what can be achieved when diverse political forces come together with a singular purpose—to defend the idea of India. Through painstaking negotiations, strategic compromises, and coordinated efforts, the alliance demonstrated that with combined efforts, a shared commitment to win, and a willingness to set aside the fight for a bigger slice of the pie, we could defeat even the most formidable adversary like the BJP. The seat-sharing process, though often fraught with difficulties, ultimately brought about unexpected successes and pivotal moments of collaboration. This alliance taught us many valuable lessons, the most important of which was this:

Rahul's unwavering dedication to the idea of an alliance, even if it meant securing zero seats in some states, exemplified the selfless vision that resonated across the partnership. This spirit of unity, shared by our alliance partners, became the foundation that cemented the INDIA Alliance.

The journey of the alliance proved that even in the face of overwhelming odds, collective resolve and a common purpose can redefine the political landscape and inspire hope for a better future. The lessons learnt from this experiment in unity should serve as a lasting reminder that with shared vision and trust, we can continue to preserve and strengthen the soul of India. I hope that this belief in collective action persists and that vested interests do not prevail to weaken the bonds we have forged.

FOUR

A NEW ERA OF CAMPAIGNING

Elections were announced in mid-March after PM Modi quickly inaugurated the first round of projects. As the ruling party began its campaign, it obviously had a decade of anti-incumbency to contend with, tall promises like ₹15 lakh in every bank account remaining unmet and explained away as *jumlas*.[1] There was also a lingering sense of PM Modi's invincibility and some remaining suspension of disbelief, not to mention measures like direct cash transfers and housing grants. Elections are a curious interplay of positive incumbency and anti-incumbency. PM Modi's boast of '*Ek akela 100 pe bhari*' passed muster, but '*Abh ki bar, 400 paar*' was his undoing.

The election campaign started on a cautious note. Spread out over seven phases and stretching over nearly two months, it was a long-haul election. In the past, the logistics of moving security forces was the main reason for spreading the election into phases. Booth capturing and election-related violence used to be endemic. Of late, the efforts of the ECI and presumably the introduction of voter ID cards and closed-circuit television have made a perceptible difference. Of course, doubts about electronic voter machines (EVMs) have not been entirely addressed, despite the ECI and the Supreme Court's repeated pronouncements upholding the integrity of digital voting.

Surprisingly, the incumbent's campaign lacked the intensity of the two previous elections but had enough energy to secure the single largest majority. Two features must be noted—the campaign did not cause the extent of communal polarization as in the previous two elections, and the RSS was not actively participating.

Right from the beginning, we knew that our adversary had the advantage of massive media backing and even on declared

---

[1] 'What About 15 Lakh In Accounts Promised By PM Modi, Asked RTI. The Reply', *NDTV*, 23 April 2018, https://tinyurl.com/2h9nazxt. Accessed on 18 November 2024.

official figures, plentiful resources, many times more than what the Congress had at its disposal. The Opposition had faith in the arithmetic of togetherness, but, of course, we all know that chemistry makes all the difference. In the run-up to the INDIA Alliance, we were very conscious of the need for chemistry, as indeed during the seat-adjustment talks. Yet, the backroom or war room interconnectivity level between partner party headquarters was somewhat limited. Fortunately, we were all naturally on the same page regarding the most important issues.

The Congress campaign for the general elections, which began with the Udaipur Chintan Shivir, and continued through the Bharat Jodo Yatra right up to the Bharat Jodo Nyay Yatra, eventually translated into a remarkable document—Nyay Patra, under the stewardship of P. Chidambaram. The guaranteed format of the manifesto was successfully used in the Telangana campaign and adapted for the national campaign.

As the political landscape in India grew ever more charged, Congress made a bold move to rally its supporters. The party unveiled an innovative crowdfunding initiative named Donate for Desh on 18 December 2023. The digital campaign drew inspiration from Mahatma Gandhi's Tilak Swaraj Fund, tapping into the rich history of India's struggle for independence. On its debut, the campaign was met with an enthusiastic response, amassing ₹1.25 crore in donations. The momentum of this initiative continued to build, capturing the imagination and support of people nationwide. By the end of its run, the campaign had successfully raised a total of ₹20 crore. Recognizing the evolving needs of this movement, on 20 January the Congress rebranded the initiative as Donate for Nyay. This new phase aimed to reinforce its commitment to the principles of justice and equality, aligning with its broader vision for the nation.

On 28 December 2023, Congress launched its Hain Taiyaar

Hum (We Are Ready) campaign in the vibrant city of Nagpur. The rally was a grand spectacle, summoning party workers from across the states to unite in a show of strength and readiness for the battles ahead.

The Hain Taiyaar Hum campaign and the successful crowdfunding effort marked a significant chapter in the Congress party's journey. As we marched forward, the party's leadership and workers drew strength from the past while looking ahead with determination, ready to face the future challenges.

Facing the Most Important Election of Our Lifetime

In the run-up to the elections, our strategy was clear—focus on 183 key seats of the 328 contested. With an impressive force of five lakh booth-level agents (BLAs) mobilized, the groundwork was meticulously laid out.

In a strategic move to strengthen our grassroots network, the party divided all Lok Sabha seats into five distinct clusters. Each cluster comprised approximately 1,000 dedicated volunteers tasked with disseminating the party's message across the country. These volunteers worked tirelessly, ensuring that the party's vision and goals reached every corner of their respective regions.

TABLE 1

Cluster 1	Telangana, Karnataka, Tamil Nadu, Kerala, Lakshadweep, Puducherry
Cluster 2	Andhra Pradesh, Maharashtra, Goa, Odisha, Andaman and Nicobar Islands
Cluster 3	Gujarat, Madhya Pradesh, Chhattisgarh, Rajasthan, Delhi, Daman and Diu, Dadra and Nagar Haveli

Cluster 4	Uttar Pradesh, Uttarakhand, Haryana, Himachal Pradesh, Punjab, Chandigarh, Jammu and Kashmir, Ladakh
Cluster 5	Bihar, Jharkhand, West Bengal, Assam, Arunachal Pradesh, Manipur, Mizoram, Meghalaya, Nagaland, Tripura, Sikkim

At the heart of this operation were the parliamentary constituency (PC) coordinators, who oversaw the efforts of volunteers in each constituency. These PC coordinators played a crucial role ensuring the dissemination efforts were well-organized and effective. They, in turn, reported to state coordinators, who managed operations at a broader level, providing guidance and support to the PC coordinators in their jurisdiction.

To ensure seamless monitoring and coordination, the Congress party established a centralized monitoring system in Delhi. From this nerve centre, the progress and activities of the constituencies were meticulously tracked. In Tamil Nadu, Karnataka and Telangana, the monitoring efforts were localized, with operations being conducted from their respective state capitals. This decentralized approach allowed for more nuanced and efficient management of dissemination efforts in these southern states.

◆

By late 2023, the political climate indicated a growing public desire for an alternative to the BJP government, with diminishing faith in its leadership. In response, the Congress party, during a series of high-level meetings focused on strategizing for the general elections, decided to establish its National War Room—a centralized command centre to coordinate campaign efforts across the country, oversee legal strategies, and ensure that it was prepared for any challenge in the upcoming election. This marked the beginning of a well-coordinated campaign machinery designed to address the aspirations of a public seeking change, while ensuring a smooth and compliant electoral process.

The Congress leadership announced the formation of the war room under the leadership of Sasikanth Senthil. Senthil, a former IAS officer who had resigned in protest against the CAA, brought a wealth of experience from his work with civil society groups and his understanding of administrative structures. His background in governance and activism made him the ideal candidate to lead the war-room effort. One of Senthil's early contributions was his involvement in the Rajasthan assembly elections, where his leadership and administrative skills played a significant role. His work in the state helped lay the foundation for the broader strategy that would be applied nationally in the general elections. Senthil's success in managing the complexities of a state election provided valuable insight into the operational framework of the National War Room.

The war room, filled with young talent from some of India's most prestigious universities, including Delhi University, Jawaharlal Nehru University and Jamia Millia Islamia, was constantly buzzing with energy. K.K. Shastri, the party's national coordinator for social media and digital platforms and in charge of Gujarat's social media, was tasked with managing these eager young volunteers.

They played a crucial role in shaping the digital outreach strategy, helping to curate content and design creatives that resonated deeply with the younger electorate. Their youthful perspective and creativity brought fresh ideas to the campaign. Each day was a whirlwind of activity, with the students brainstorming, creating and designing content aimed at captivating the attention of Gen Z. Their efforts ensured that the party's message was not only heard but also embraced by first-time voters across the country.

One evening, during a break, Jairam Ramesh walked into the

war room for a meeting. Seeing the bustling room full of young faces, he couldn't help but quip, 'Shastri, you've converted this war room into a Youth Congress office.' The hall erupted in laughter, everyone recognizing the compliment behind his words. It was a moment of light-heartedness that underscored the importance of the youth's contribution to the campaign.

The war room also assessed the party's strengths and weaknesses, aiming to prepare it for the general elections. Despite the benefits of its decentralized structure, the Congress Party faced the challenge of efficient coordination required to run a national election campaign.

The war room was restructured to operate at the village level, with each unit named a Sathi Kendra, designed to foster a sense of belonging among the villagers. The idea was to create teams that worked in sync with each other while maintaining a seamless connection with the central war room through state and parliamentary coordinators. Constant engagement with the volunteers on the ground was made possible through WhatsApp and Zoom meetings.

One night, when the former chief minister of Rajasthan, Ashok Gehlot, connected with the volunteers from the village, a moment of unexpected warmth unfolded. An emotional volunteer handed his phone to his wife, saying, 'You always say no one in the party cares for me, but look, here is CM Sahab himself, calling me at this late hour.' His voice brimmed with pride as he shared the moment with her. In another village, a young woman eagerly showed off her scooter, her face glowing excitedly. 'This was given to me by Gehlot Sahab under the Rajasthan government's policy for girls,' she explained, her voice exuding gratitude.

The strategic clustering and hierarchical reporting structure exemplified the Congress party's commitment to a highly organized, far-reaching campaign. By leveraging the dedication of thousands of volunteers and meticulous oversight of coordinators, the party was able to create a robust network that could effectively spread its message and galvanize support across the nation. As the campaign unfolded, this structured approach proved to be the cornerstone of our strategy, underscoring the importance of organization and grassroots engagement in our political journey.

The efforts of the war room were bolstered by a cohesive campaign strategy orchestrated by seasoned leaders like K.C. Venugopal, the party's general secretary, and Ajay Maken, the party's treasurer, at 11 Talkatora Road, which became the nerve centre of publicity operations. Their task was not just to disseminate the party's message but also to ensure it resonated deeply with voters across the targeted constituencies.

Supriya Shrinate spearheaded the social media campaign, leveraging platforms to engage voters directly and amplify the party's narrative beyond the traditional media channels. At 10 Rajesh Pilot Marg, the hub for media operations, strategies were crafted to maintain a favourable narrative in the press.

In the communications war room, Vaibhav Walia and his team of dedicated volunteers, including Vineet Punia, Amitabh Dubey, Mohammed Ali and Supriya, vigilantly monitored the strategies of opposition leaders, including PM Modi, Amit Shah and J.P. Nadda. Their objective was clear—to intercept, counter, and ensure the party's message not only reached the voter base but also penetrated deep into it.

Randeep Surjewala and Manish Chatrath meticulously managed the star campaigners, including Mallikarjun Kharge, Rahul and Priyanka Gandhi. Their rallies and public appearances were systematically planned to maximize impact and connect with diverse voter demographics.

In the run-up to the election campaign and through the period of seven phases, it was the communications department, headed by the irrepressible Jairam Ramesh, ably supported by Pawan Khera and Supriya Shrinate and all the party spokespersons, that took on the BJP spokespersons and Amit Malviya, word by word and phrase by phrase, besting them at every step. If our top leadership confidently and courageously took on the BJP, the communications department would keep up the fight in the media and social media. The vicious reality the BJP media warriors sought to create was given a fitting reply through virtual (and virtuous) reality.

Long before the results, it was clear that the social media space was at least an equal battle, unlike the 'Godi media' territory where subservience to the ruler was glaring.[2] Credit must of course be given to independent YouTubers and the digital media reportage by icons like Ravish Kumar, Ajit Anjum, Abhisar Sharma, Dhruv Rathee and Saurabh Dwivedi.

Leveraging Symbolism, Emotion and Everyday Experiences

Twenty years ago, we defeated the BJP's 'India Shining' campaign with the Aam Admi Ko Kya Mila initiative, shifting focus from *gareeb* (poor) to *aam admi* (common citizen), believing that people did not like to be called poor. We were elected to form a government in 2004—the UPA I—led by Dr Manmohan Singh.

In the 2024 electoral campaign, Congress revisited this strategy with a series of bite-sized ads designed to ignite intrigue and capture public attention. Due to the paucity of time, we decided to focus our efforts on a positive campaign centred around the Congress INC rather than indulging heavily in negative campaigning. Our strategy was to personalize the

---

[2]Iyer, S. Aishwarya, 'Is India's free press not so free after a decade of Modi?', *CNN*, 22 May 2024, https://tinyurl.com/44kf6yt5. Accessed on 14 January 2025.

campaign with phrases like *Hath badlega halaat* (The hand will change the situation), *Judega Bharat, Jeetega INDIA* (India will unite, INDIA will win), and *Nyay ka haq milne tak* (Until the right to justice is achieved). Slogans like *Mere vikas ka do hisaab* (Give me the account of my development) asked voters to reflect on how the government's policies directly benefited them. This approach allowed us to connect with the electorate on a personal level, making the campaign more relatable and impactful.

At the heart of these campaigns was a bold and innovative approach that leveraged symbolism, emotion and everyday experience, often reminiscent of consumer advertising tactics. By blending political critique with relatable storytelling, we aimed to galvanize support and position ourselves as agents of change. Bite-sized ads were used to amplify this message. For instance, one ad depicted a distraught woman in a vegetable market, grappling with rising prices and economic strain, lamenting, *'Jo bhi khareedne jaun sab mehenga hai. Ghar kaise chalaun. Mere Vikas ka do hisaab.'*[3] (Whatever I go to buy is expensive. How should I run my household? Give me an account of my development.) This scene resonated deeply with voters facing economic hardships, framing the election as a choice between continuity and change. In another ad, a young engineering graduate, reluctantly shedding his professional attire to drive a rickshaw due to unemployment, questions the efficacy of government initiatives like Make in India and Startup India. *'Engineering ke last year se hi pata tha ki life toh set hai. Suna hai Make in India aur startups desh ko aage bada rahe hai. Aur jab desh aage bad raha ho toh ek pada likha thodi piche rahega. Bola gaya tha karodon ko rojgaar milega, par*

---

[3] Indian National Congress, https://tinyurl.com/bd37f7tm. Accessed on 9 December 2024.

milega ye, ye nahi pata tha. Mere Vikas ka do hisaab.[4] (Since my final year of engineering, I was confident that life was set. I have heard that Make in India and startups are driving the country forward. And when the country is progressing, an educated person can't lag behind. We were told that millions would get jobs, but no one mentioned what kind of jobs we would get. Give me an account of my development.)

Recognizing the importance of visibility, we quickly identified and secured advertisement slots during the Indian Premier League (IPL). We capitalized on these prime slots to broadcast our ads, ensuring our message reached a broad and diverse audience. Notably, the BJP did not have any ads running on IPL slots at that time, giving us a significant advantage in terms of visibility. However, this advantage was short-lived. After our campaign made waves, the IPL eventually changed its policies, leading to the cessation of political ads during the matches.

These narratives underscored the party's campaign theme encapsulated in its slogan, *Hath badlega halaat*, symbolizing its commitment to addressing socioeconomic challenges and offering an alternative vision for the future. As the election drama unfolded, these innovative strategies left a lasting impression on the electorate, shaping the discourse and anticipation surrounding the Lok Sabha polls.

Our creative spin on political commentary not only garnered attention but also effectively conveyed our narrative on governance failures. During a notable, possibly the first of its kind, press conference, Congress spokesperson Pawan Khera demonstrated the manner in which several figures previously associated with the Congress and its allies had crossed over to the BJP despite allegations of corruption and scrutiny by investigative

---

[4]Indian National Congress, https://tinyurl.com/2pwn9esc. Accessed on 9 December 2024.

agencies like the Enforcement Directorate (ED) and the Central Bureau of Investigation (CBI). Their cases were either closed or simply disappeared from the public space.⁵ Khera used a visual demonstration involving a white t-shirt emblazoned with accusations like scam, corruption and fraud. Placed inside a contrived 'BJP washing machine', the shirt emerged with its dark allegations rearranged to read 'BJP Modi Wash', symbolizing the party's strategy of rebranding controversies into a palatable narrative.⁶ This theatrical critique not only highlighted the BJP's tactic of cleaning its image but also alluded to the perceived hypocrisy of welcoming individuals with tainted reputations into its fold. Adding another layer of irony, a poster resembling a detergent ad prominently featuring PM Modi's face alongside the words 'Modi washing powder' in Hindi evoked amusement.⁷

Our relentless efforts at highlighting the Modi government's failures received a shot in the arm on 15 February when the Supreme Court struck down the Electoral Bond Scheme as unconstitutional. This was a pivotal moment; it validated our long-standing concerns and shed light on the government's opaque dealings. The court's directive to make the data public brought forth revelations that directly corroborated our allegations. We had consistently argued that the electoral bonds system was not the transparent reform it was claimed to be, but rather a tool to conceal the flow of political funds, allowing for unchecked quid pro quo arrangements between corporations and the ruling party. With the Supreme Court's order, the data began to tell the story

---

⁵'23 of 25 Opposition leaders accused of corruption got reprieve after joining BJP since 2014: Report', *Mint*, 3 April 2024, https://tinyurl.com/487h5j7e. Accessed 14 January 2025.
⁶'Washing machine on dais, Congress taunts BJP over 'clean chit' to leaders aligning with ruling party', *Indian Express*, 30 March 2024, https://tinyurl.com/9y3ahb4s. Accessed on 18 November 2024.
⁷Ibid.

we suspected all along—one of hidden donors, concealed motives, and a government bent on controlling the narrative.

Once the data was made public, it was analyzed extensively by journalists and political analysts. The deputy chairman of the war room, Varun Santosh, was quick to set up a team comprising Rayan Sud, a young Standford graduate, and members of the party's research departments to analyze the data. What they discovered was nothing short of explosive. Several instances of quid pro quo between the corporate world and the BJP emerged.

Jairam Ramesh released a series of tweets highlighting these findings and exposing the Modi government, using the now-viral term PayPM—a play on the popular digital payment app PayTM—to criticize PM Modi's government. In one of his tweets, Ramesh noted, 'To give the exact numbers, 33 loss-making companies donated ₹434 crores to the BJP via Electoral Bonds!'[8] This revelation raised questions about why loss-making firms would donate such large sums.

Ramesh followed up with a detailed breakdown of the #PayPM scam, asserting that the BJP had looted ₹4 lakh crore of public money.[9]

> Pre-paid bribes: *Chanda Do, Dhanda Lo*
> Post paid bribes: *Theka Lo, Rishvat Do*
> Post-raid extortion: *Hafta Vasuli* through ED/IT Raids
> Farzi Companies

Investigative reports, such as the one by *The Hindu*, corroborated Ramesh's claims. Their research revealed that at least 20 newly incorporated companies, likely shell companies, had purchased

---

[8] @Jairam_Ramesh, *X* (formerly Twitter), 8 April 2024, 4:22 p.m., https://tinyurl.com/49p8ckwk. Accessed 14 January 2025.
[9] @Jairam_Ramesh, *X* (formerly Twitter), 11 April 2024, 8:03 p.m., https://tinyurl.com/49p8ckwk. Accessed 14 January 2025.

electoral bonds worth ₹103 crores, even though existing laws prohibited companies less than three years old from making political donations.[10] The Modi government, however, had systematically dismantled the rules that previously regulated corporate donations. One of the most significant changes was removing the provision that capped corporate donations at 7.5 per cent of the company's average net profit from the past three years.[11] This, coupled with the complete anonymity offered to donors through electoral bonds, created a murky system that obscured the source of political funds and undermined public accountability.

Both the ECI and the RBI had warned as early as 2017 that the electoral bonds scheme could lead to the use of black money and facilitate money laundering through shell companies.[12] Despite these warnings, the Modi government moved forward with the scheme, overruling the objections of both institutions.[13]

Ramesh tweeted, 'The Modi *sarkar* (government) overruled their objections, presumably to ensure the steady flow of *chanda* (donations).'[14] He bitterly noted that the ECI and RBI's warnings were indeed prophetic. With each passing day, new dimensions of the PayPM scam surfaced, exposing how the government had allegedly enabled and perpetuated a corrupt political-funding structure.

---

[10] Radhakrishnan, Vignesh, and Parthasarathy Sambhavi, 'At least 20 firms bought electoral bonds within 3 years of incorporation, a punishable offence: Data', *The Hindu*, 10 April, Accessed on 18 November, 2024 https://tinyurl.com/59yecnbz. Accessed on 18 November 2024.
[11] Ibid.
[12] Ibid.
[13] 'Electoral bonds: Govt ignored red flags raised by Reserve Bank, Election Commission', *The Indian Express*, 22 November 2019, https://tinyurl.com/bddzke2y. Accessed on 24 December 2024.
[14] @Jairam_Ramesh, X (formerly Twitter), 10 April 2024, 9:57 a.m., https://tinyurl.com/49p8ckwk. Accessed 14 January 2025.

In the run-up to what Ramesh described as 'the most important election of our lifetime', the revelations about electoral bonds and corporate quid pro quos cast a long shadow over India's political landscape.[15] The return of the electoral bonds scheme, as declared by Nirmala Sitharaman, promised a continuation of what Ramesh called 'loot'—a direct assault on the transparency and integrity of the democratic process.[16]

Resilience amid Roadblocks

Rahul Gandhi, at the forefront of this movement, strategically leveraged social media platforms to connect directly with the masses and the party base. Emphasizing personal engagement and transparency, he bypassed traditional media to speak directly to the people, fostering a sense of immediacy and authenticity in his communication.

His direct communication and innovative use of social media not only amplified his reach but also cemented his position as a dynamic and influential leader. His popularity soared, making him the most favoured candidate for PM amongst the opposition with 27 per cent support, according to a CSDS survey.[17] As the election campaign progressed, his digital presence flourished. *India Today* reports highlighted that Rahul had gained more new followers on YouTube and Instagram than PM Modi during the election period. His YouTube subscribers skyrocketed from five million to a staggering eight million, while his Instagram followers

---

[15]'Congress attacks FM Sitharaman over her 'electoral bonds will be back' remark,' *Hindustan Times*, 20 April 2024, https://tinyurl.com/yc5vshcf. Accessed on 18 November 2024.

[16]Ibid.

[17]'Bharat Jodo Yatra Effect? Rahul Gandhi's approval rating surges, emerging as strong contender alongside PM Modi: Report', *Mint*, 24 May 2023, https://tinyurl.com/2wp87nnd. Accessed on 18 November 2024.

surged from 1.7 million to 10.4 million.[18]

The impact of his digital strategy was profound. According to an *ABP News* report on 16 May, the Congress manifesto, heavily influenced by Rahul Gandhi in style and content, was downloaded 8.8 million times.[19] This unprecedented engagement underscored the manifesto's resonance with the public and highlighted Rahul's pivotal role in shaping the party's vision and message.

As the campaign progressed towards its culmination, Rahul injected fresh energy with his *khata-khat* refrain, which the workers quickly picked up as a rallying cry. As the election drew near, the enthusiasm and momentum generated by his efforts were palpable, marking a significant chapter in the Congress party's storied history.

Priyanka Gandhi emerged as a formidable force on the campaign trail. Her extensive campaign efforts saw her participating in 108 public meetings and roadshows. She gave 100 media bites, appeared in a television interview, and gave interviews to five print publications. Her relentless campaign spanned sixteen states and one union territory, a testament to her dedication and tireless energy.

Priyanka's connection with the grassroots was palpable, especially during her two worker conferences in Amethi and Rae Bareli. In Rae Bareli, she passionately said, '*Yeh woh zamin hai jahan mere aur aapke purvajon ka khoon pasina mila hai... hamare liye ye desh ki sabse pavitra mitti hai...ham isko sirf apne liye nahi balki apne gaon, sheher, prant...aur desh ke har nagrik ke swabhiman ke liye bachayenge.*' (This is the land where our

---

[18]Sharma, Aakash, and Shubham Tiwari, 'PM Modi, Rahul Gandhi or Arvind Kejriwal: Who won social media game this election', *India Today*, 31 May 2024, https://tinyurl.com/Modi-social-media. Accessed on 14 January 2025.
[19]Kumar Singh, Ashish, 'Lok Sabha Elections 2024: Rahul Gandhi hits on social media! Congress manifesto gets 88 lakh downloads', *ABP News*, 16 May 2024, https://tinyurl.com/4p9ued2p. Accessed on 18 November 2024.

ancestors toiled with blood and sweat for the national interest. This is the most pious piece of land for us, and we shall save it for the self-respect of every citizen in the country.)[20] Her words resonated deeply, invoking a sense of shared heritage and collective responsibility to protect the land for future generations.

Priyanka's presence and persuasive rhetoric left an indelible mark on the electorate. Her speeches, public engagements and unwavering commitment to the party's cause invigorated the Congress campaign, injecting it with renewed vigour and hope. 'She looks like Indira Gandhi' resonated throughout the campaign. Despite crores spent by the Modi campaign and the advent of social media, Indira Amma remains part of the folklore of Indian politics, particularly in the South and in tribal belts.

The fruits of Priyanka's labour became evident on election day. Of the 43 seats where she had campaigned, the Congress secured victory in 20 seats, marking a success rate of 46.5 per cent.[21] This impressive outcome underscored her campaign effectiveness and ability to galvanize support. Just as our campaign began gaining momentum, we hit a major roadblock. Our bank accounts in which money donated by people had been kept were frozen by the BJP-led NDA government. This was an attempt by the BJP to deprive the Congress of a level-playing field in the elections.[22] Congress treasurer Ajay Maken explained how the party's eleven accounts in four banks were frozen. 'For a notice for financial

---

[20]Sharda, Shailvee, 'With fiery speech, Priyanka Gandhi Vadra takes Amethi, Rae Bareli charge', *The Times of India*, 7 May 2024, https://tinyurl.com/ydydh4ur. Accessed on 9 December 2024.

[21]Handa, Aakriti, 'Election Result 2024: Congress Won 46% Seats Where Priyanka Gandhi Campaigned', *The Quint*, 6 June 2024, https://tinyurl.com/Priyanka-Gandhi-wins. Accessed on 14 January 2024.

[22]'"Don't have money": Mallikarjun Kharge alleges BJP froze Congress bank accounts', *India Today*, 14 March 2024, https://tinyurl.com/mu5th5su. Accessed on 24 December 2024.

year 2017–18, a lien on ₹210 crore was marked in our eleven accounts in four banks. The reason given was that ₹14.49 lakh was received in cash (as donations made by our MPs to the Congress party) out of a total receipt of ₹199 crores. This cash is just 0.07 per cent of the total donations. And the punishment was 106 per cent.'[23] He further informed that the party had received a notice from the Income Tax Department for a financial year as far back as 1993–94 (when Sitaram Kesri was treasurer) and was asked to calculate penal charges after 31 years of assessment.[24]

Maken insisted that the timing of this action raised serious questions. 'We received the ₹199 crore donation in 2017–18, but after seven years, on 13 February 2024, ₹210.25 crore lien was marked, our bank accounts were virtually sealed, and later, ₹115.32 crore was forcibly confiscated,' he remarked.[25]

With all our bank accounts frozen just before the elections, we were unable to do any campaign work or even support our candidates. They failed to take flights; in fact, they found it difficult even to purchase a rail ticket for the campaign.

Commenting on the manner in which our ability to fight the elections was severely damaged, Rahul insisted that even though the institutions were tasked with safeguarding the democratic framework, the ECI and the judiciary remained silent. He explained why the idea that India is the world's largest democracy is a lie. 'This is a criminal action on the Congress Party done by the prime minister and the home minister. This type of activity does not happen without them in today's India [...] Twenty per cent of India votes for us, and we are not

---

[23]'In rare presser with Kharge and Rahul, Sonia Gandhi alleges "systematic effort by PM to cripple Congress financially"', *Indian Express*, 22 March 2024, https://tinyurl.com/54bcmjjs. Accessed on 19 November 2024.
[24]Ibid.
[25]Ibid.

able to pay ₹2 for anything [...] Even if our bank accounts are unfrozen today…a huge amount of damage has been done to Indian democracy.'[26]

After considering legal avenues, Congress concluded that the most effective approach would be communicating directly with the public through nationwide press conferences, highlighting how the party was being denied a level-playing field.

Five Pillars of Our Policy Agenda

Beyond press conferences, the party realized that the best way to engage directly with voters was through the party manifesto. In March, the CWC convened an extensive session to deliberate on the party manifesto. Over more than three hours, the party leaders and members of the CWC engaged in robust discussions to finalize the manifesto's key promises and strategies. On 5 April, the Congress party released its comprehensive manifesto for the 2024 Lok Sabha elections, titled 'Nyay Patra: Paanch Nyay and Pachees Guarantee'.[27]

At its core, the '5 Nyay 25 Guarantees' package embodied a commitment to social justice and inclusive development. It comprised a robust set of policies designed to uplift the marginalized, empower women, bolster healthcare, enhance education, and provide economic security to all citizens. Each guarantee was meticulously tailored to resonate with the aspirations and needs of diverse communities across India. The significance of this welfare package extended beyond electoral promises; it

---

[26]'In rare presser with Kharge and Rahul, Sonia Gandhi alleges "systematic effort by PM to cripple Congress financially"', *Indian Express*, 22 March 2024, https://tinyurl.com/54bcmjjs. Accessed on 19 November 2024.
[27]'Nyay Patra – Lok Sabha Elections 2024', Indian National Congress, https://tinyurl.com/c3d395xa. Accessed on 19 November 2024.

encapsulated a vision for a progressive India where no citizen would be left behind. By articulating clear, actionable policies, the Congress party aimed not only to win votes but also to lay the foundation for sustainable and inclusive growth.

The five *nyay*s of the Nyay Patra were:

> *Yuva Nyay* (Youth Justice)
> *Naari Nyay* (Women Justice)
> *Kisan Nyay* (Farmer Justice)
> *Shramik Nyay* (Worker Justice)
> *Hissedari Nyay* (Participatory Justice)

The guarantees under each nyay included:

Yuva Nyay aimed to empower the youth with promises like *Bharti Bharosa*, which proposed creating 30 lakh new central government jobs. *Pehli Naukri Pakki* guaranteed the right to an apprenticeship with a public or private sector company for all educated youth, providing a stipend of rupees one lakh per annum. To address exam paper leaks, the Congress party pledged to enact stringent laws to eradicate such incidents completely, establish fast-track courts for swift adjudication, and provide monetary compensation to the victims. The Gig Economy Mein Samajik Suraksha Guarantee sought to improve working conditions and provide social security for gig workers. *Yuva Roshni* promised ₹5,000 crore in startup funds to support and nurture the entrepreneurial spirit of the youth.

Naari Nyay focused on women's empowerment and justice. The Mahalakshmi Scheme promised one lakh rupees to each poor household, with the oldest woman of the household receiving the amount. The Adhi Abaadi, Poora Haq scheme promised 50 per cent reservation for women in new central government jobs. Under the Savitribai Phule Hostels plan, the number of hostels for working women would be doubled. The Shakti Ka Samman programme aimed to double the salaries of ASHA, Anganwadi and midday meal workers.

Kisan Nyay concentrated on justice for farmers. The Sahi Daam programme promised a legal guarantee for the MSP based on the Swaminathan formula. Karz Maafi Aayog proposed the establishment of a Standing Loan Waiver Commission for farmers. The GST Mukt Kheti initiative aimed to eliminate GST on farming inputs.

Shramik Nyay addressed the rights and welfare of labourers. Shram ka Samman promised a national minimum wage of ₹400 per day, including for MGNREGS workers.

Hissedari Nyay emphasized social equity and inclusion. The Ginti Karo guarantee aimed to conduct a caste census to provide an accurate socioeconomic picture. The Aarakshan Ka Haq guarantee promised to remove the 50 per cent cap on Scheduled Castes (SC), Scheduled Tribes (ST) and Other Backward Classes (OBCs) reservations, and to fill up the full backlog of SC, ST and OBC jobs. Jal-Jangal-Zameen Ka Kanuni Haq aimed to settle Forest Rights Act, 2006, claims within a year.

In past campaigns, despite the well-crafted manifestos that resonated with the aspirations and needs of the citizens, they were not utilized to their fullest potential. Most promises were shared primarily through social media, but the party soon realized the limitations of relying solely on this strategy. The over-reliance on social media has not yielded the desired results. Recognizing the importance of timely and direct engagement with voters, the party decided to implement a more focused strategy—delivering the manifesto door to door.

However, distributing a full copy of the manifesto to every household was not feasible due to the significant costs involved, especially as the party's accounts were frozen. To address this, pamphlets were distributed. These pamphlets were to be printed by the state units and the candidates themselves, with the design provided by the central team.

The manifesto team and the communications department worked closely to distil the manifesto's promises into 5 Nyays. Much time was spent meticulously choosing the font size and images to ensure the pamphlets were visually appealing and easy to understand.

The Indian Youth Congress (IYC), under the leadership of its national in-charge, Krishna Allavaru, mobilized its members to distribute the manifesto effectively. Allavaru adopted a multi-pronged approach to maximize the reach of the manifesto's promises. He began by decentralizing the campaign and clustering the seats into three categories: 1) borderline seats, 2) seats with strong candidate coordination, and 3) borderline seats with strong candidates. He focused his efforts on the first two categories. To support this large-scale operation, he established four war rooms in the key cities of Delhi, Chandigarh, Bangalore and Hyderabad. The design of the manifesto pamphlet was also strategic. The front page highlighted the 5 Nyays, while the back page was customized with promises tailored to each candidate's area and state, ensuring that each candidate had a personal incentive to distribute the manifesto in their constituency.

Technology played a crucial role in streamlining and monitoring the reach of the manifesto. An incentive-based structure was created, with targets and points awarded based on performance. A feedback system was integrated into the campaign app to ensure members of each household accepted the manifesto. Recipients were encouraged to call a designated number and press a button from one to five, indicating which nyay appealed to them the most. This feedback system not only boosted the campaign team's confidence but also provided real-time data on the manifesto's reach.

On social media, the IYC used artificial intelligence to customize campaigns, focusing on the last-mile localized narratives. Youth Congress workers were carefully selected for these tasks from its vast database of members, with their performance in previous campaigns assessed using a ladder-based system. Initiatives like Shakti Clubs and Indira Fellowship were launched to involve women in the Youth Congress and women aspiring to enter politics. Shakti Clubs operated at the IYC level, while Indira Fellowship was a parallel entity supported by the IYC. Both initiatives aimed to create platforms for first-time women political activists who were not from political families. These groups were also tasked with distributing the manifesto using the same ladder-based incentive structure. A dedicated team assessed the performance of the members involved in these initiatives.

Through a strategically planned and carefully executed campaign, IYC reached out to two crore households and connected with 30 lakh people registered on the app. The app also provided valuable insights, revealing that Nari Nyay was the most popular nyay, followed by Yuva Nyay—Pehli Naukri Pakki. This was not achieved magically; there was a clear push from Rahul to Nari Nyay. Behind this was a strategically designed campaign by Vaibhav Walia, Manish Sharma and Krishna Allavaru, who involved Dr Akriti Bhatia, a PhD scholar from Delhi School of Economics specializing in urban and informal labour politics. She organized various meetings among women in working-class clusters.

Powerful narratives and insights from the field emerged from these meetings, highlighting the resounding support and participation of women voters mobilized around Nari Nyay. At one of these meetings, a local woman remarked, '*Dulha aur chulha bohot ho gaya. Hamare bhi armaan hai, pehchan hai. Ab hamein barabari ka samman chahiye. Naari Nyay guarantee is disha mein ek sahi aur sacha prayas hai.*' (We have lived in the shadow of our husbands in the kitchens for a long time. We, too, have aspirations and identities. We now want equal respect and standing in society. Nari Nyay guarantee is the right and true step in this direction.)

The Nari Nyay guarantee campaign, wherever it reached successfully, struck a personal chord with women voters, who began to appeal to other women for support with a very unusual campaign pitch. As one woman campaigner identified at these meetings emphasized: 'I am not asking you to vote for the Congress party because you will benefit from their schemes. I am asking you to vote for the Congress because of me. I will be able to use this one lakh for my younger son's coaching fee. I don't have to beg my husband for this fee. My elder son will get another one lakh as a stipend in his first apprentice job. Therefore, if you want to help yourself, vote for the Congress and tell other women the same too!'

In addition to these gatherings organized by the IYC, numerous other meetings were organized throughout the campaign period to directly engage with the public on the promises outlined in the manifesto. These gatherings were not mere formalities but crucial platforms for detailed discussions on the five nyays—the key pillars of our policy agenda. Each interaction was meticulously designed to ensure clear communication and understanding, aiming to bridge the gap between political promises and the public's expectations.

The Congress leadership, including Rahul and Priyanka Gandhi, actively participated in these engagements, emphasizing their commitment to addressing pressing issues the electorate faced. From rural villages to urban centres, the Nyay Patra was presented as a blueprint for inclusive growth and social justice, resonating with voters across demographics.

This proactive approach marked a departure from traditional campaign tactics, focusing not just on rhetoric but also on genuine dialogue and accountability. By actively disseminating and discussing the manifesto's contents, Congress aimed to build trust and credibility among voters, showcasing their readiness to govern with transparency and diligence.

As the election day approached, the impact of this strategy became evident. Not only were voters aware of the Congress party's promises, but they also felt empowered by their direct engagement in the democratic process. This grassroots approach to manifesto delivery exemplified a new era of political campaigning in India, where responsiveness to public concerns and proactive communication were prioritized, reshaping the dynamics of electoral politics.

Caste Census: A Defining Feature of 2024

As the campaign gained momentum and it became increasingly clear the political wind was shifting, Rahul began carrying a copy of the Constitution wherever he went. This symbolic gesture was not just a random decision; it was a carefully considered move suggested by Amitabh Dubey, who oversaw research and monitoring in the Congress's media and communications department. Amitabh believed that carrying the Constitution would serve as a powerful reminder of the values and principles that the Congress party stood for, particularly at a time when those very principles seemed to be under threat.

The idea struck a chord with Rahul, who immediately saw its significance. Jairam Ramesh had a well-preserved pocket-sized copy of the Constitution in his office, which he offered to Rahul. This copy soon became Rahul's constant companion, tucked in his pocket during speeches, meetings and public appearances.

Soon enough, saving democracy morphed into saving the Constitution; the oft-repeated phrases began to take the shape of a solemn obligation. Our campaign to preserve and protect the Constitution was to ensure that the noble agreement between the people of India must not be violated. Beyond that, Nyay's commitment was to ensure that the entitlements underscored in the text of the Constitution would be delivered to the citizens on the ground.

In addition to saving the Constitution, Rahul championed the caste census as the cornerstone of his political mission. The issue emerged as a central issue in our campaign.

This initiative, deeply rooted in longstanding demands from OBCs and SCs, aimed to rectify historical inequalities and amplify the voices of marginalized groups. The last caste-based census in India had taken place in 1931, and despite previous attempts, such as the 2011 proposal led by Congress leader and former union minister M. Veerappa Moily, efforts had faced numerous obstacles.[28] Internally, Congress encountered resistance, especially from senior leaders who feared pushing the caste agenda might alienate upper-caste voters. In the end, a compromise was reached, allowing a caste census to be conducted alongside the decadal census, though its results were never made public due to concerns about the statistical reliability of the data.[29]

After the 2019 election results, discussions around the caste census intensified between Rahul and members of civil society, along with intellectuals advocating for greater social justice and

---

[28] Ghildiyal, Subodh, 'Moily writes to PM with demand for caste-based census', *The Times of India*, 15 September 2009, https://tinyurl.com/3e252wxk. Accessed on 24 December 2024.
[29] Chatterji, Saubhadra, 'Why the 2011 caste data was not made public?', *Hindustan Times*, 30 August 2024, https://tinyurl.com/2fkrjaw5, Accessed on 24 December 2024.

representation. These conversations underscored how the BJP had strategically relied on OBC and SC voters to bolster its electoral strength while simultaneously marginalizing them from meaningful positions of power.[30]

Rahul began pushing for a caste census during internal party discussions, viewing it as a critical tool to rectify the underrepresentation of marginalized communities and directly challenge the BJP's dominance among these voter blocs. His advocacy of the caste census not only demonstrated his commitment to empowering OBCs, SCs and other disadvantaged groups, but also became a pivotal element in shaping Congress's strategy to reclaim its standing in Indian politics. By making caste census a central issue, Rahul aimed to realign the party's focus to social equity and inclusivity, offering a powerful counter-narrative to the BJP's tactics.

The Congress party's push for a caste census gained momentum through Rahul's strident championing. To this end, background support was provided by key party seniors and organizational support from the Samruddha Bharat Foundation (SBF), an organization committed to furthering the constitutional idea of India. The SBF was pivotal in laying the groundwork for the census by advocating for policy reforms across the UPA and then in the INDIA parties. In December 2021, the SBF organized a national OBC conclave where the idea of caste census was openly discussed, although Rahul did not attend this event. The conclave was intended to be a launchpad for a national push towards caste census but Congress political strategists had advised postponing the initiative due to the Uttar Pradesh assembly elections. The SBF further strengthened the cause by organizing events in cities

---

[30] Arnimesh, Shankar, et al., '"Sabka Saath" in BJP cabinets, but plum portfolios still with "upper, dominant" castes', *The Print*, 7 March 2023, https://tinyurl.com/BJP-cabinets. Accessed on 14 January 2025.

like Lucknow, Panchkula and Delhi, where Rahul consistently advocated for the census, bringing the issue to the forefront of Congress's campaign.

As a result, the issue continued to gather support within the Congress. Key events, such as the Udaipur Chintan Shivir in May 2022 and the eighty-fifth Congress plenary session in Raipur in February 2023, ensured that the issue remained a focal point of discussion. At the Raipur session, Rahul linked the caste census to the legacy of Jawaharlal Nehru, emphasizing its importance in understanding the true demographic representation of India's marginalized communities and addressing their needs more effectively. It was clear that the caste census was no longer merely a political tool for Rahul but had become his personal 'life mission'. His vision was bold: To bring attention to the 90 per cent of the population he claimed had been left out of the system and create a more inclusive India.

It was in 2023 that the CWC unanimously endorsed the caste census, marking a significant shift in the party's internal strategy.

In line with the party's broader commitment to social justice, Mallikarjun Kharge and Rahul Gandhi had taken a significant step by amending Section VI A of the Congress party's constitution, removing the cap on caste-based reservations within the party.[31] This move aligned the party's internal policies with its external advocacy for equitable representation of the SC, ST and OBC population. This amendment had sparked considerable debate within the party. Some voices had expressed concern about the potential consequences of such sweeping changes. However, Rahul had remained resolute, defending the move as essential to creating a more balanced and representative Congress. By pushing for the caste census and removing reservation caps, Congress presented

---

[31] Indian National Congress, 'The Congress Constitution', https://tinyurl.com/INC-constitution-document. Accessed on 14 January 2025.

itself as a party committed to uplifting disadvantaged communities and reshaping India's electoral system to make it more inclusive.

However, the push for the caste census was not without resistance. The party faced opposition from within the political landscape and from the government. Efforts to stifle the conversation about the caste census, including media suppression, were evident.[32] Yet, alternative media outlets and grassroots movements had surged, suggesting that the public, particularly marginalized communities, were increasingly receptive to the idea despite attempts to silence them.

The demand for caste census and the campaign surrounding constitutional reforms had a noticeable impact on voting patterns across India, reshaping the political landscape in favour of Congress. As the elections drew nearer, the reverberations of Rahul's steadfast commitment to caste census and the party's broader push for social equity could be seen in the way various communities, particularly the OBCs, SCs and other marginalized groups, began to gravitate towards the Congress in key states.[33] [34]

Historically, these communities were divided in political allegiances, often courted by regional parties and even the ruling BJP in previous elections. However, the empowerment narrative woven around the caste census resonated deeply with these groups, many of whom had long felt sidelined in the national discourse. The Congress's campaign had rekindled a sense of hope among

---

[32] 'Congress leader Anand Sharma opposes party's demand for caste census', *The Times of India*, 21 March 2024, https://tinyurl.com/Anand-Sharma-Congress. Accessed on 14 January 2025.

[33] Sharma, Samrat, and Ashish Ranjan, 'INDIA bloc gains OBC votes but still lags, exit poll shows', *India Today*, 2 June 2024, https://tinyurl.com/y93z6rzj. Accessed on 14 January 2025.

[34] Ranjan, Ashish, '"Constitution in danger": Why Dalits voted against BJP in Lok Sabha', *India Today*, 9 June 2024, https://tinyurl.com/mtmedb82. Accessed on 14 January 2025.

them, offering a vision that directly addressed their concerns about representation, access to resources, and acknowledgement of their rightful place in India's complex social fabric.

In Uttar Pradesh, where caste politics has always played a decisive role, the Congress's promise of a caste census struck a powerful chord. Voters from the OBC and SC communities, who had previously aligned with the BSP and the BJP, began to shift their loyalties to the INDIA bloc.[35] The Congress's focus on caste-based representation offered what these parties had struggled to deliver—a voice for their communities. The party seemed to offer a comprehensive plan that could translate into meaningful policy change. In the heartland of Hindi-speaking India, this momentum had not only weakened the grip of the BJP but also created a new electoral reality for the Congress.

In the western and southern states, where the BJP had made significant inroads in the previous elections, the caste census narrative proved a formidable counterweight. In Maharashtra, Karnataka and Tamil Nadu, the push for the caste census triggered a shift among communities that had traditionally viewed Congress with scepticism. The Congress's campaign had deftly linked the caste census to the larger issue of constitutional reforms, presenting it as a critical step toward safeguarding the rights of marginalized groups. By focusing on a constitutional framework that could remove the reservation cap and ensure greater representation, Congress had signalled that it was not merely posturing but also intent on delivering systemic change.

In Karnataka, for instance, the Lingayat and Dalit communities, which the BJP had aggressively courted, began to view the Congress

---

[35] Shekhar Singh, Indra, 'Ground Report: The Tide Has Turned Against BJP Across Caste Groups in UP', *The Wire*, 27 May 2024, https://tinyurl.com/dwpwdyz8. Accessed on 24 December 2024.

as a more reliable advocate of their long-term interests.[36] The Congress's strategy of building alliances with smaller caste-based groups, while promoting the idea of a nationwide census that would accurately reflect their numbers and needs, had reawakened a sense of political urgency. The shift in voting patterns became particularly evident in rural areas, where the caste census was seen not just as an abstract idea but as a tangible promise of improved socioeconomic conditions.

The impact of Congress's caste census campaign was perhaps most pronounced in Rajasthan and Haryana—states where the electoral balance had historically swayed between the Congress and the BJP. Here, Congress traditionally drew its strength from upper-caste communities, but the party's focus on caste equity through the census led to a broadening of its base. In these regions, the lower-caste groups, particularly STs and OBCs, began to view the Congress as the only party committed to breaking the cycle of underrepresentation. This shift in allegiance was reflected in the electoral outcomes, where a significant portion of the OBC and SC vote bank moved towards the Congress, eroding the BJP's once-dominant hold.[37] [38]

As the election results unfolded, the ripple effects of this caste census campaign became clear. The Congress's ability to position itself as a champion of marginalized communities, advocating for their rights not only rhetorically but also with a clear constitutional

---

[36]Sukumaran, Ajay, 'How Congress won back Lingayat support in Karnataka', *India Today*, 27 May 2023, https://tinyurl.com/ycx3rz5p. Accessed on 24 December 2024.

[37]Ranjan, Ashish, '"Constitution in danger": Why Dalits voted against BJP in Lok Sabha', *India Today*, 9 June 2024, https://tinyurl.com/mtmedb82. Accessed on 14 January 2025.

[38]Sharma, Samrat, and Ashish Ranjan, 'INDIA bloc gains OBC votes but still lags, exit poll shows', *India Today*, 2 June 2024, https://tinyurl.com/y93z6rzj. Accessed on 14 January 2025.

agenda, reshaped the political map in several states. The voting patterns showed a clear shift—where these communities were once fragmented or loyal to regional parties and the BJP, they had begun to coalesce around the Congress banner. This realignment, driven by the demand for a caste census and the promise of constitutional reforms, underscored how deeply the idea had penetrated the political consciousness of these voters.

The caste census became more than just an electoral issue—it became a symbol of the Congress's broader fight for inclusivity and representation. The changing voting patterns in various states served as a testament to the power of this narrative and its capacity to influence political behaviour at the national level. The Congress's push for the census had rekindled its relationship with its old voter blocs, and the results were a striking affirmation of Rahul's long-term vision to rebuild the party on the principles of social equity and justice.

The success of the caste census campaign was driven by the efforts of K. Raju, a former IAS officer and Rahul's close aide. With his vast experience in policy and governance, Raju was instrumental in crafting the campaign's core messages. His close relationship with Rahul had allowed him to align the goals of the caste census with the party's broader vision of social justice and inclusivity. It was this alignment that made the campaign so effective.

Rajesh Lilothia, Chairman of the Congress SC Department and a seasoned leader known for his grassroots work with marginalized communities, ensured that the message was not lost in political rhetoric but reached the ground, connecting directly with the SC, ST and OBC communities. He built vital connections, ensuring that the voice of the caste census resonated where it was needed most.

Kancha Ilaiah, a respected intellectual and fierce advocate of caste equity, had provided the intellectual foundation for the campaign. His deep understanding of caste dynamics and social justice reinforced the narrative, positioning the caste census as an essential tool for addressing deep-rooted inequalities.

Together, this trio formed a cohesive and highly efficient team. They had transformed what could have remained a distant political promise into a dynamic movement that sparked discussions across the country. Their strategy not only raised awareness but also deeply engaged the communities most affected by caste-based disparities. This had driven significant grassroots support and reinforced the Congress party's long-standing commitment to social justice. Through its leadership, the caste census had become more than just a political issue; it evolved into a rallying point for marginalized groups, energizing the Congress campaign and advancing the call for a more inclusive and representative India. Their collective efforts solidified the party's position as a champion of the underrepresented and underserved, making the caste census a defining feature of the 2024 elections.

FIVE

FIGHTING THE POLITICS OF FALSEHOOD

Not surprisingly, the BJP and PM Modi had very little to say about the issues raised by the INDIA Alliance or even about their record in office. Their biggest professed achievement, the construction of the Ram Temple, failed to get them the Ayodhya seat in the elections. Meanwhile, the BJP candidates sought 400 seats to 'amend the Constitution', presumably to abolish reservations.[1] It is another matter if they cannot handle their people on the streets, as in the case of periodic lynching on grounds of religion or allegedly dealing with beef.[2][3][4][5][6]

PM's Poll Pitch: Misreading Intent, Misleading Suggestions

PM Modi and his campaign speeches often left the listeners speechless. In addition to repeating the name of Lord Ram, the PM engaged in unexpectedly crude remarks about intruders, individuals with many children, those who would snatch away

---

[1] Salaria, Shikha, '"Need 2/3rd majority to change or make new Constitution"—BJP Ayodhya MP's remark sparks row', *The Print*, 14 April 2024, https://tinyurl.com/2ujkxfn4. Accessed on 27 December 2024.

[2] Daniyal, Shoaib, 'The Modi Years: What has fuelled rising mob violence in India?', *Scroll.in*, 23 February 2019, https://tinyurl.com/yc4eewfy. Accessed on 14 January 2025.

[3] 'Local BJP leader among 11 convicted in Alimuddin Ansari lynching case in Jharkand', *CJP*, 16 March 2018, https://tinyurl.com/ycxv2epp. Accessed on 14 January 2025.

[4] Ghatwai, Milind, 'Madhya Pradesh: BJP leader arrested for 'provoking' mob involved in Dhar lynching', *The Indian Express*, 7 February 2020, https://tinyurl.com/3br4td5k. Accessed on 14 January 2025.

[5] Singharia, Kanishka, 'Caught on camera, Rajasthan BJP leader talks of lynching: "My supporters killed"', *Hindustan Times*, 20 August 2022, https://tinyurl.com/3wvntcmx. Accessed on 14 January 2025.

[6] Pal Singh, Ravish, 'One of the accused in Madhya Pradesh mob lynching case is local BJP leader: Congress', *India Today*, 6 February 2020, https://tinyurl.com/mvxhhvpf. Accessed on 14 January 2025.

women's *mangalsutra*s (sacred thread), take their buffaloes, and unscrew the faucets on water pipes.[7] The PM's provocative statements were fact-checked widely. Of course, some deference is shown to people in high office, but even patience and understanding have limits. Clearly, Goebbels' strategy of repeating a lie enough times to make it appear the truth was at work. Fortunately, the country was discerning enough not to be swayed by the falsehood.

In an interview with Navika Kumar of *Times Now*, PM Modi addressed concerns about socioeconomic conditions among Muslims, calling for reflection on why certain communities have not fully benefited from government schemes during the Congress regime.[8] It turned out to be a rare occasion when the PM refrained from his appeasement-attack mode.

During his poll rally in Banswara, Rajasthan, on 21 April, the PM claimed that when Congress was in power, 'They said that Muslims had the "first right" to the nation's wealth. This means that if Congress comes to power, it will confiscate people's *bhain*s (buffaloes), land, money, mangalsutra gold, and redistribute to infiltrators and families with more children. Should your hard-earned wealth be given to infiltrators? Do you accept this?'[9]

What about the law of the land, the rule of law, one might ask. And indeed, why buffaloes?

A fact-check by *Scroll* on positions that PM Modi confidently

---

[7]'PM Modi doubles down on anti-Muslim rhetoric, says "Congress wanted to give SC-ST quota to Muslims"', M*int*, 23 April 2024, https://tinyurl.com/5e6m2zrr Accessed on 27 December 2024.
[8]Narendra Modi, '"Na Hum Islam ke khilaaf hai, Na Musalmaan," PM Modi busts Congress' false narrative', *YouTube*, https://tinyurl.com/2rxh4w7p. Accessed on 14 January 2025.
[9]Narendra Modi, 'PM Modi Live | Public meeting in Banswara, Rajasthan | Lok Sabha Election 2024', *YouTube*, https://tinyurl.com/yj7xv7u3. Accessed on 14 January 2025.

held during the campaign, starting with the Banswara rally, merits being reproduced here:[10]

> **Claim:** Modi claimed that the Congress manifesto said it would survey, seize, and redistribute private wealth, including the mangalsutras of married Hindu women.
>
> **Fact:** [Obviously], the Congress manifesto contains no reference to private property being confiscated, let alone the mangalsutras of women.

But the insidious innuendoes are obvious, making it unbecoming of a person in high office.

> **Claim:** Modi went on to claim that the previous Congress government had said Muslims have the first right to the country's resources.
>
> **Fact:** This is a distortion of a speech delivered in 2006 by Manmohan Singh when he was prime minister. He had spoken about the need to uplift all disadvantaged sections in India, including Scheduled Castes, Scheduled Tribes, Other Backward Classes, women and children, not just religious minorities.

Of the latter, he underscored Muslims who, according to the Sachar Committee Report, were at the bottom of the social pyramid. A fact-check by *The Quint* on the same claims made by PM Modi mentions the following:

> While speaking about "collective priorities", former PM Singh had remarked on the need to develop several sectors—

---
[10]Barnagarwala, Tabassum, and Abhik Deb, 'Fact-checking five days of Narendra Modi's speeches: A catalogue of lies', *Scroll,* 28 April 2024, https://tinyurl.com/mvktv85n. Accessed on 21 November 2024.

like agriculture, irrigation, water resources, health, education and others. These sectors needed development, "along with programmes for the upliftment of SC and STs, other backward classes, minorities, and women and children. We will have to devise innovative plans to ensure that minorities, particularly the Muslim minority, are empowered to share equitably in the fruits of development. They must have the first claim on resources," Singh said. With this, it becomes clear that former PM Singh had stressed on the importance of prioritizing plans and schemes which work towards uplifting Scheduled Castes (SC), Scheduled Tribes (ST), other backward classes, women, children, and minorities, and not just the Muslim community.[11]

From the poll rally in Banswara, the *Scroll* then fact-checked the claims made by the PM in his other rallies.[12]

Claim: Modi next claimed that the Congress would distribute the wealth among 'infiltrators' and 'those who have more children.'

Fact: [...] the Modi government had repeatedly told Parliament that it had no data on illegal immigrants. The fertility rate of Indian Muslims, although higher than Hindus, is declining faster than that of all other communities. Besides, fertility is a function of economics, not religion. For instance, Muslims in more-developed Tamil Nadu have fewer children than Hindus in poorer Bihar.

---

[11] Varma, Aishwarya, 'Did Ex-PM Singh Say Muslims Have 'First Right' to Wealth as PM Modi Claimed?', *The Quint*, 22 April 2024, https://tinyurl.com/mryzbpcw. Accessed on 21 November 2024.

[12] Barnagarwala, Tabassum, and Abhik Deb, 'Fact-checking five days of Narendra Modi's speeches: A catalogue of lies', *Scroll*, 28 April 2024, https://tinyurl.com/mvktv85n. Accessed on 21 November 2024.

Aligarh, 22 April

Claim: Modi repeated the false claim that the Congress manifesto threatened to survey and seize private property. 'The *shahzada* (prince) of Congress'—a reference to Congress leader Rahul Gandhi—'has said if the party comes to power, a survey will be conducted to find out how much income, property, wealth, houses you have…The manifesto says the government will seize and redistribute property.'

Fact: The Congress manifesto certainly does not say this. At the launch of the manifesto on 6 April, Rahul Gandhi said, 'We will do an x-ray of the country. Backward classes, Dalits, Adivasis, poor people belonging to the general category, and minorities will get to know what their share is in the country.'

That is a reality check, not intent to deprive any citizen. The Congress believes that course corrections in affirmative action can only be done with sufficient data.

Claim: Modi went on to claim: 'The Congress will go to the extent that if you have an ancestral home in your village, and you have purchased a small flat in the city for your children, it will snatch one of them away… Isn't this Maoist thinking? The Congress wants to snatch your hard-earned wealth; it wants to loot women's property.'

Fact: The only reference to redistribution in the Congress manifesto is this: 'Congress will establish an authority to monitor the distribution to the poor of government land and surplus land under the Land Ceiling Acts.'

Surely this is not simply a case of misreading intent but of misleading suggestion.

Tonk-Sawai Madhopur, 23 April

Claim: Bringing up the x-ray reference from Rahul Gandhi's speech, Modi said, 'This means that if there is a box in your home in which you store bajra grain, even that would be subjected to an x-ray. All your property that is found to be more than what you need it will be seized and redistributed. If you have two houses, and they spot that in their x-ray, one will be taken over by the government. Is this acceptable to you?'

Fact: Neither in the Congress manifesto nor in the speeches of its leaders is there any reference to the government seizing and redistributing people's homes.

The Constitutional scheme does not permit such far-fetched actions. Instead, the BJP leadership must answer questions about bulldozer injustice perpetrated in their ruled states.

Sagar, 24 April

Claim: Modi claimed that in Karnataka, the Congress had instituted reservations on the basis of religion through illegal means. 'Through a single notification, it included all Muslim communities in the OBC quota. The Congress snatched away a big part of OBC reservations and gave it on the basis of religion.'

Fact: In 1962, the Congress government in Karnataka included certain castes of Muslim communities in the list of Other Backward Classes, not on the basis of religion, but on the recommendation of the R. Nagana Gowda Commission.

Later, in 1994, the H.D. Deve Gowda-led Janata Dal (Secular) government brought all Muslim communities in Karnataka under the OBC list, carving out a four per cent sub-quota for them. The

Janata Dal (Secular) is currently an ally of the BJP.

Gujarat, where Modi was chief minister for 12 years, also lists Muslim communities among OBCs. In an interview with ANI two years ago, Modi had boasted about seventy Muslim castes getting reservation benefits in the state.

Surguja, 24 April

Claim: Modi said that the Congress had first attempted to implement reservations based on religion in Andhra Pradesh, and planned to implement the same quota across the country. 'They proposed a 15 per cent quota on the basis of religion,' he said. 'They also proposed that some people should be given reservation on the basis of religion by curtailing, stealing away from the existing quota for SCs/STs and OBCs. The Congress expressed this intention in its manifesto in 2009. In the 2014 manifesto, too, they clearly said that they will never leave this matter.'

Fact: The Congress government in Andhra Pradesh passed a law in 2005, providing five per cent reservation to Muslims. The High Court struck down the law as unconstitutional, arguing that religion cannot be 'the sole basis for determining a class of citizens as socially backward.'

However, subsequently, upon satisfying the backward requirements, OBC Muslims were allowed the reservations and benefitted enormously.

In its 2009 manifesto, the Congress adopted a careful line, saying it was committed to giving reservations for minorities 'on the basis of their social and economic backwardness.' Its 2014 manifesto said, 'The Indian National Congress is committed to finding a way forward for introducing reservation in education and employment for economically weaker sections of all communities without in any way affecting existing reservations for Scheduled Castes, Scheduled Tribes and Other Backward Classes.'

Instead of junking the data of the Sachar Committee and the Ranganath Misra Commission Reports, PM Modi should address the concerns expressed there. If religion alone cannot be the basis for affirmative action, it cannot also be a ground for reverse discrimination. Let us not forget that his government is committed to *Sabka Saath, Sabka Vikas, Sabka Vishwas* (Together with everyone, development for everyone, trust of everyone).

Claim: In the same speech, Modi repeated the claim that in Karnataka the Congress had implemented a quota based on religion. 'When the BJP came to power in the state, we scrapped the Congress's decision that was against the Constitution and the ideals of Babasaheb Ambedkar and gave the Dalits and Adivasis their rights back,' he said.

Fact: In March 2023, the BJP government in Karnataka scrapped the four per cent sub-quota for Muslim OBCs. But it did not reallocate the quota to Dalits and Adivasis. Instead, it transferred it to the state's dominant communities, the Lingayats and the Vokkaligas. The order was stayed by the Supreme Court in April 2023, observing that it was prima facie fallacious.'

Claim: Modi then introduced another claim: 'The Congress is saying it will impose inheritance tax; it will even tax the wealth inherited from parents. Your children will not get the wealth that you accumulate, and the Congress will snatch it away from you.'

Fact: The Congress manifesto does not contain any reference to an inheritance tax. All it says is: 'We will address the growing inequality of wealth and income through suitable changes in policies.'

Tax statutes are responsive to the changing circumstances, and responsible politics does not permit ad hoc, pre-conceived positions.

Betul, 24 April

Claim: Modi claimed that the Congress wanted to snatch away reservations from SC, ST and OBC groups to give them to a *khaasam khaas* (special) vote bank. Repeating claims about Congress extending religion-based reservations to Muslims, he said the party was plotting to seize and redistribute private wealth to 'strengthen its vote bank'.

Fact: The Congress manifesto neither talks about religion-based reservations nor about the redistribution of wealth.

However, the '400 *paar*' refrain was repeatedly projected by BJP leaders as intended to fundamentally alter the constitutional schemes and take away reservations. The Dalits punished the BJP in response.

Claim: Returning to the subject of an inheritance tax, Modi claimed that Congress was lying when it said that the idea of imposing such a tax was merely the 'personal opinion' of Sam Pitroda. 'The truth is that in 2011, Congress had advocated inheritance tax,' he said.

Fact: In 2011, P. Chidambaram, home minister at the time, had mooted the idea of an inheritance tax. But the Congress is not alone in considering the move. In 2017, Arun Jaitley, the finance minister in the first Modi-led BJP government, also toyed with the idea.

There are two views on such a tax on many fiscal provisions, but the country has not expressed a view on this, and it remains on the shelf. Scientific approach to life and resorting to emotional attitude will remain a challenge for modern democracy, underscoring the need for electoral education about societal responsibility.

Agra, 25 April

Claim: Modi claimed that the Congress planned to steal a part of the 27 per cent quota for OBCs to give reservations on the basis of religion.

Fact: The Congress manifesto does not contain any reference to religion-based reservations.

Of course, people of all religions can be and are OBCs. One backward community identified by occupation cannot be treated differently from another similarly placed community because of a different faith.

Claim: Modi first claimed that Congress planned to seize 55 per cent of people's inheritance, then argued that 'the assets you are bequeathing to your next generation, more than half would be taxed.'

Fact: The Congress's manifesto contains no reference to an inheritance tax.

Self-created phantoms are put to use to subvert choice and obscure the performance record of the government.

Morena, 25 April

Claim: Repeating the false claims about reservations for Muslims in Karnataka, Manmohan Singh's speech, and the Congress snatching mangalsutras, Modi returned to the subject of inheritance tax. This time, he made a novel claim: 'When Indira Gandhi died, and her son Rajiv Gandhi was to inherit her property, to ensure the government did not get the money, to save the property, the prime minister Rajiv Gandhi abolished the inheritance tax.'

Fact: What was abolished in 1985 by V.P. Singh, then finance minister, was estate duty levied on the assets of a deceased person.

No attempt was made to propose estate duty or inheritance tax afresh, although such provisions are known to apply in law in the USA, from where Sam Pitroda might have got the idea. But Congress never adopted the idea.

Aonla, 25 April

Claim: After running through the usual set of false claims about the Congress surveying and taking away people's property, Modi added: 'Not just an economic survey, the Congress aims to survey all institutions, all offices. If it finds any backward class or Dalit family has two members holding jobs, then the Congress will snatch away one and give to those (read Muslims) who they think have the first claim to the country's resources.'

Fact: The party's manifesto states: 'Congress will conduct a nationwide socioeconomic and caste census to enumerate the castes and sub-castes and their socioeconomic conditions. Based on the data, we will strengthen the agenda for affirmative action.'

Sitapur, Uttar Pradesh, 5 May

Addressing a rally in support of BJP candidate Rekha Verma in Dhaurahra, PM Modi said that the poor and those belonging to the SC, ST and OBC communities also came to the BJP.

> **Claim:** 'Muslim brothers and sisters are seeing that (houses under) PM housing scheme were given to all the needy. Be it water connection or gas cylinder under Ujjwala Yojana, every government benefit was given to all...they (Muslims) are also getting benefits of all schemes without discrimination,' PM Modi said.[13]
>
> He added that the manifesto of the Opposition reflects the Muslim League's thinking. 'Now, to save the Muslim vote bank, these people (Opposition) are playing a new game and are out doing appeasement in the open,' he insisted. He pointed out that B.R. Ambedkar and even Jawaharlal Nehru had said clearly that there would be no reservation on the basis of religion, and said the Congress and INDIA bloc were 'adamant on giving reservation on the basis of religion.'[14]
>
> **Fact:** PM Modi's claim that the Opposition wants to abolish reservations and give it to Muslims is an absurd idea.[15] Backward Muslims in Mandal OBC category get reservations, and not Muslims per se.

---

[13] "'I Urge The Muslim Community To...'": PM Modi Warns Against Religious Divide For Political Gain', *News 18*, 7 May 2024, https://tinyurl.com/4v6kx6p3. Accessed on 27 December 2024.

[14] 'Muslim community understands Congress, INDIA bloc using them as pawns, says PM Modi', *The Hindu*, 5 May 2024, https://tinyurl.com/mrx7yuba. Accessed on 22 November 2024.

[15] Kulshreshtha, Saurabha, 'Congress to cut SC, ST, OBC quota to give it to Muslims: Amit Shah in Maharashtra', *Hindustan Times*, 10 November 2024, https://tinyurl.com/3xmjyjk9. Accessed on 27 December 2024.

I do not know what the definitive view of the Sangh Parivar is with regard to minorities in general and Muslims in particular. It is one thing to resort to negative suggestions about Muslims for political gain, quite another to honestly believe that Muslims are unwanted as citizens of India, and if they must live here, they must conform to an exclusive, majoritarian India.[16] [17] [18] Such talk is heard from people in high places as well, and some tolerate or even acquiesce in it.[19] [20] However, it has never been officially declared as state policy.

For the past few decades, Muslims have been somewhat cautious in supporting the Congress because of the backlog of events relating to Babri Masjid and recurring communal riots. There has been much reflection since 2014 and the advent of the BJP government. Although over the years it has become politically incorrect to publicly focus on the Muslim vote, perhaps for strategic reasons rather than an ideological shift of focus to PDA (Pichda, Dalit, Alpsankhyak), this election has reconnected mainstream parties with Muslims. This election saw a surge of support from ordinary Muslims, the first of its kind in over two decades. Key religious leaders took the initiative to sway opinion in favour of the Congress and the INDIA Alliance, as did group

---

[16] Barton, Naomi, '10 Times When BJP Leaders (Not Fringe) Made Anti-Muslim Hate Speeches', *The Wire*, 6 June 2022, https://tinyurl.com/yn9jd3h9. Accessed on 15 January 2025.

[17] Truschke, Audrey, 'How India's Hindu Nationalists Are Weaponizing History Against Muslims', *Time*, 6 October 2023, https://tinyurl.com/bde7yfj3. Accessed on 15 January 2025.

[18] Mander, Harsh, 'India: no country for Muslims', *South China Morning Post*, 17 December 2017, https://tinyurl.com/mr22nfpm. Accessed on 15 January 2025.

[19] 'PM Modi made Islamophobic remarks in 110 campaign speeches: Human Rights Watch', *The Hindu*, 14 August 2024, https://tinyurl.com/yec5pezw. Accessed on 15 January 2025.

[20] Meer, Faisal, 'Muslim MP called 'terrorist, pimp' by BJP member inside India's parliament', *Al Jazeera*, 22 September 2023, https://tinyurl.com/58pesdx2. Accessed on 15 January 2025.

initiatives like Indian Muslims for Civil Rights. Members led by former MP Mohammad Adeeb travelled across the length and breadth of the country.[21] There is a new sense of urgency among these eminent personalities to engage the Congress in a dialogue for the road ahead.

As a result, parties like Asaduddin Owaisi's AIMIM remained confined to its core area of Hyderabad, while the Peace Party of India virtually disappeared. Maulana Badruddin Ajmal's outfit in Assam, the All India United Democratic Front, suffered a crippling blow when the leader himself lost Dhubri by over ten lakh votes to Congress party's Rakibul Hussain.

Prime Minister Modi's freewheeling diatribe was not limited to his rivals in the Opposition. Sometimes, even friends were not spared.

> In a public meeting on 8 May in Telangana's Karimnagar, he asked, 'अंबानी–अडानी से कितना माल उठाया है. काले धन के कितने बोरे पैसे मारे हैं, क्या टेंपो भरकर नोट कांग्रेस के लिए पहुंचे हैं? क्या सौदा हुआ है?'[22] (The tempos loaded with money known to the PM of the country, and not a finger lifted by the ED and CBI!)

However, of all the statements, what took the cake was the PM's assertion to a media channel that he realized after his mother's death that he was not biologically born but had been sent by God to serve the people.[23] Why this became apparent on his

---

[21] Wajihuddin, Mohammed, 'Mumbai: Muslim leaders to campaign for civil rights', *The Times of India*, 19 July 2022, https://tinyurl.com/yc35wn4z. Accessed on 27 December 2024.

[22] Narendra Modi, 'PM Modi addresses a public meeting in Karimnagar, Telangana', *YouTube*, https://tinyurl.com/ba339jru. Accessed on 14 January 2025.

[23] 'PM Modi invites ridicule for saying he is not biological, but "sent by god"', *The News Minute*, 23 May 2024, https://tinyurl.com/h54wuju5. Accessed on 21 November 2024.

lamented mother's demise is far from clear, and why many eminent personalities perform God's mission without claiming non-biological character might be a point to ponder. Thankfully, we did not encounter this claim again, although we must live with the thought that it might resurface in the future.

The *Parivaarvaad* Paradox

Yet, what surfaced repeatedly during the campaign was the obsession of the BJP's top leadership with the idea of the Nehru-Gandhi dynasty in politics. Every adverse event was and continues to be twisted to blame it on them; many ideas of history are glossed over to pass them off as meant for the personal gratification of the family. Much is read into the choice of constituency. As a matter of fact, innumerable leaders in the Congress owe aspects of their careers to dynasties. But equally, if not more, the shoe fits the BJP for its homegrown candidates and those they have poached from the Congress. A quick, random glance at the lineup of BJP leaders is an eye-opener, as indicated in this article by Louise Khurshid.[24]

> A big song and dance is being made of the so-called dynastic overreach of the Gandhi/Nehru family by the powers that be in the BJP. As if Jawaharlal Nehru, like a phoenix, rose from his ashes and 'anointed' first his daughter Indira Gandhi, then his grandson Rajiv Gandhi, and now his great-grandson Rahul Gandhi. As if Indira Gandhi had no trial by fire and, by sheer guts and the genius of her political acumen, did not squash the Syndicate of S. Nijalingappa, K. Kamaraj, Atulya Ghosh, S. K. Patil and N. Sanjeeva Reddy to form the Congress (I). As if

---
[24]Khurshid, Louise, 'Dynasty everywhere', *The Indian Express*, 15 September 2018, https://tinyurl.com/3thtuyfv. Accessed on 22 November 2024.

Rajiv Gandhi did not win Lok Sabha elections from Amethi in Uttar Pradesh to repeatedly become an elected MP. And as if Rahul Gandhi parachuted down from nowhere to become Congress president and did not, like his father, actually fight and win repeated elections to the Lok Sabha.

As if Anurag Thakur is not the son of the former Chief Minister of Himachal Pradesh and did not descend on the political scene because of the dynastic groundwork laid out by his father. As if Dushyant Singh was a local grassroots level worker and not the son of the Chief Minister of Rajasthan when he stood for Lok Sabha from his mother's pocket borough of Dholpur. As if Rajbir Singh and now his son Sandeep inherited no dynastic legacy from former chief minister and [then] Governor Kalyan Singh. As if Maharashtra Minister Pankaja Munde and her sister Pritam and their cousin Poonam Mahajan did not inherit the dynastic cloak of their late fathers, Gopinath Munde and Pramod Mahajan respectively. Just as if Varun Gandhi was not appointed a General Secretary of the BJP because he is the son of Menaka Gandhi who is the widow of Sanjay Gandhi, who was the son of Indira Gandhi and the grandson of Jawaharlal Nehru.

That is why Amit Shah and company continuously condemn Yashodhara Raje Scindia and Vasundhara Raje Scindia because they inherited the dynastic legacy of their mother, Rajmata Vijayaraje Scindia. Or do they? There was no link up with Naveen Patnaik, and he was condemned as the dynastic inheritor of the legacy of Biju Patnaik. And no truck with Chandrababu Naidu because he was the political inheritor of N.T. Rama Rao. But didn't they? Just as they condemn Akhilesh Yadav and Dimple Yadav, and Dharmendra Yadav and Tej Pratap Yadav and Ramgopal Yadav and his son Akshay Yadav as the benefactors of the patriarchal umbrella of Mulayam Singh Yadav. Or do they?

Just as they attack M.K. Stalin, M.K. Alagiri and Kanimozhi for being the political inheritors of Karunanidhi. Or do they? And just as they shun the Shiv Sena because Uddhav Thackeray took the reins from his late father, Balasaheb Thackeray, and he is encouraging his son, Aditya, to come to centre stage Shiv Sena Politics. Or do they? Just as they constantly berate Sharad Pawar for encouraging his daughter, Supriya Sule, to benefit from his clout. And they criticize Lalu Prasad Yadav for encouraging his wife, Rabri Devi, his daughter Misa, and then his sons, Tej Pratap and Tejashwi, to enter politics centre stage. Or do they? Just as Rajnath Singh's son, Pankaj Singh, doesn't mention his father in his election posters. As Shivraj Singh Chouhan's son Kartikey has no intention of following any dynastic assertion. Or doesn't he?

Just as they kept Omar Abdullah out of the Atal Bihari Vajpayee government because he was the son and grandson of Jammu and Kashmir Chief Ministers, Farooq Abdullah and Sheikh Abdullah, respectively. And similarly, they refused to make Ajit Singh a minister in any BJP-led NDA government because he inherited the political legacy of his father, Charan Singh. Or did they?

Just as they shun the Badal family of Punjab because, not just their son but daughter-in-law and several other relatives held positions of power. They now refuse to entertain a Badal daughter-in-law as a minister in the current BJP Government. Or have they? Just as they repeatedly took potshots at the generations of Chautalas because they dared inherit the political legacy of Chaudhary Devi Lal. Or did they?

Just as they discarded Agatha Sangma because she was the daughter of the late Purno Sangma. And today they have *nothing to do with Chief Minister Conrad Sangma because he, too, is a son of Purno Sangma. Or don't they?*

Just as they joined a Government with Mehbooba Mufti because they believed she inherited nothing from Mufti Mohammad Sayed.

Interestingly, they never hit out at Jyotiraditya Scindia for stepping into the shoes of late Madhavrao Scindia or Jitin Prasada for inheriting the mantle of late Jitendra Prasada or Sachin Pilot for fighting the good fight of the late Rajesh Pilot or Jagan Reddy wanting to inherit the Chief Ministership his late father Rajasekhara Reddy once had. So why is there a different yardstick for Rahul Gandhi?

Top on the list is the mother-son duo of Maneka Gandhi and Varun Gandhi, although this time the mother lost from Sultanpur, and the son was denied a ticket to contest from Pilibhit.[25] There are innumerable others. Devi Lal's son Ranjit Singh Chautala joins a list that includes family members of Lal Bahadur Shastri, Charan Singh, P.V. Narasimha Rao and H.D. Deve Gowda, who belong to either the BJP or part of the NDA. Then, of course I know I.K. Gujral's son, Naresh Gujral, has been a prominent member of the Akali Dal. In more recent times, Piyush Goyal, Anurag Thakur, Poonam Mahajan, Pankaja Munde, Devendra Fadnavis, Parvesh Sahib Singh, B.Y. Raghavendra, Jayant Sinha, Rajvee Singh, Dharmendra Pradhan, Chirag Paswan, Abhishek Singh, Kiren Rijiju, Rita Bahuguna Joshi, Pankaj Singh and Bansuri Swaraj will surely not deny their parental heritage and pedigree. In all fairness, I must declare similar attributes.

As one can see from the list, which is not exhaustive, many

---

[25]Pandey, Neelam, 'BJP's Maneka Gandhi loses to SP rival by 43,000-plus votes in Uttar Pradesh's Sultanpur', *The Print*, 4 June 2024, https://tinyurl.com/ym9awn2j. Accessed on 27 December 2024.

public figures are from the third or fourth generation. Many are highly qualified professionals who have done outstanding work in their respective sectors. What draws them to political office remains a mystery that needs to be uncovered.

We may agree with the ground reality or indeed vigorously argue for political mobility; the fact remains that this is not a legitimate political or electoral argument for any contemporary party, except for the likes of the Communist movement.

There is no ambiguity about the situation; without being judgemental, one can merely underscore the facts. In such an open-and-shut case, it would clearly be hypocrisy to utter a word about dynasties.

Matching Malice with Legal Muscle

With the elections come the Model Code of Conduct and the imperative for a level-playing field. It is, at best, an approximation, since the incumbent has an obvious advantage of power until the eve of the notification of dates of polls. Anti-incumbency presumably contributes its bit to levelling the playing field, as validated by statistics that show many sitting MPs who are not re-elected.

Either way, our public life seldom encourages a free and fair discussion of our condition. Social science scholars can profitably delve into the political reality of our times to pinpoint the peculiar mix of remnants of our feudal past and surviving tribal loyalties, interspersed with the zeal of social revolution, in contemporary politics. Periodically, the established status quo is challenged, as in the case of the emergence of the Asom Gana Parishad (AGP), the Telugu Desam Party (TDP), the BSP and the AAP, all of which were gradually absorbed into the established systems. The more things change, the more they stay the same. A fresh wave of disenchantment gives birth to an alternative dispensation or reversion to the established political parties.

Returning to the election period and the Model Code, the BJP had allegedly committed a significant number of electoral violations. While minor and infrequent violations of electoral norms are committed in all elections across the political spectrum, the eighteenth Lok Sabha elections witnessed an unprecedented increase in divisive and religiously fuelled electoral speeches. The top brass of the BJP consistently made speeches rife with communal rhetoric and baseless and malicious allegations against political opponents and religious groups.[26] These speeches served the sole purpose of polarizing the electorate and consolidating votes based on xenophobic rhetoric against the Muslim community, portraying them as conspirators who would have hegemony on the nation's resources.

As the decibels of the campaign continued to be raised, there was a need to maintain a check on electoral violations by various political parties as well as keep the house of the Congress in order. And so, a legal reconnaissance team was constituted. This was led by legal luminaries Dr Abhishek Manu Singhvi, Randeep Singh Surjewala and me. It also comprised a team of advocates—Muhammad Ali Khan, Omar Hoda, Eesha Bakshi, Uday Bhatia, Arjun Sharma and Kamran Khan. This legal team worked closely with Ranjith Kumar and Nishant Patil from the party's social media team. The team was responsible for scouring all major social media platforms to identify potential instances of violations by political parties, their members, or other third parties. This information was then supplied to the legal team to initiate legal action.

---

[26] Rauf, Shyma, "'Mullahs & Mangalsutras': A look at "hate speeches" in Indian politics in recent history', *Deccan Herald*, 31 May 2024, https://tinyurl.com/4e4d7rcy. Accessed on 14 January 2025.

Upon receipt of the information, we prepared and submitted memorandums and representations in the form of complaints to the ECI, containing (a) the exact offence committed, (b) the individuals involved in committing the offence, and (c) jurisprudence on the offence laid down by the courts of the country.

Once prepared, the complaints were submitted to the ECI with an in-person delegation of the party led by Singhvi, Surjewala and me. Depending on the issue, we would be accompanied by senior and regional party leaders to provide a comprehensive explanation of the on-ground and real-time impacts of the reported violations.

The complaints we filed were mainly against the BJP's utter disregard for the rule of law, be it for its incorrect, misleading, and false narratives pertaining to the Congress echoed on various social media handles or for its incendiary speeches that evoked religious sentiments, exacerbating communal differences and pitting communities against each other.

We also filed a complaint against PM Modi for making outrageous and deplorable claims against the Congress and the Muslim community at a public rally in Banswara, Rajasthan, on 21 April, calling the latter *ghuspathiye* (infiltrators).[27] The rhetoric of the speech made at Banswara became the central narrative that featured in the speeches of the senior BJP leaders. Amit Shah and Yogi Adityanath also made speeches in the same tenor as the PM.[28] [29] Overall, we filed fifteen complaints against PM Modi, seven against Yogi, and three against Shah.

---

[27]Chakrabarty, Sreeparna, 'We are looking into complaint against PM Modi's Rajasthan speech: Election Commission', *The Hindu*, 24 April 2024, https://tinyurl.com/upk6wht6. Accessed on 27 December 2024.

[28]'Yogi Adityanath rakes up Ayodhya firing to attack Dimple Yadav amid mangalsutra row', *India Today*, 25 April 2024, https://tinyurl.com/ytz4ffst. Accessed on 27 December 2024.

[29]'India: Hate Speech Fueled Modi's Election Campaign', *Human Rights Watch*, 14 August 2024, https://tinyurl.com/528nez2f. Accessed on 27 December 2024.

However, despite irrefutable evidence that their speeches violated the law, the ECI took no action against the blatant violations of electoral norms by BJP leaders.[30][31] Even with respect to complaints filed against other prominent leaders such as Anurag Thakur, Smriti Irani and Himanta Biswa Sarma, the ECI took no action.[32]

Even as an alliance partner, we coordinated three multi-party delegations, comprising leaders from Opposition parties, to present INDIA Alliance's collective grievances before the ECI.

All in all, we filed 122 representations on eight occasions between 16 March and 4 June—averaging close to three complaints a day—regularly apprising the ECI of violations of electoral norms and seeking clarifications with respect to directions issued by the Commission.

Even after the polling of votes was concluded, the legal reconnaissance team remained operational, actively reporting incidents of possible violations to the ECI. In fact, even on counting day on 4 June, we filed several representations before the ECI about reports of non-adherence to the procedure for counting of votes and violations of the Conduct of Elections Rules, 1961, and even addressed the said issues during an in-person hearing before the ECI on that very day itself. For instance, we raised concerns about the slow pace of vote counting in numerous polling centres across Uttar Pradesh and Bihar.[33] On the ground

---

[30]Joy, Shemin, 'Lok Sabha Elections 2024: EC's refusal to take direct action for 'communal' remarks by top leaders dents credibility', *Deccan Herald*, 22 May 2024, https://tinyurl.com/2b6dvuxx. Accessed on 15 January 2025.
[31]Devasahayam, M.G., 'The 2024 Lok Sabha Election is a Tale of Egregious Errors and Wanton Violations', *The Wire*, 20 June 2024, https://tinyurl.com/ym947475. Accessed on 15 January 2025.
[32]PTI, 'LS polls: Cong MP files complaint against Assam CM over MCC "violation"', *Business Standard*, 10 April 2024, https://tinyurl.com/5n86xhdh. Accessed on 15 January 2025.
[33]'Congress submits memorandum to ECI over slowing down of counting',

in Uttar Pradesh's Bansgaon, our workers relayed distressing accounts of intimidation and obstruction faced by their counting agents.[34] These incidents, highlighted to the Commission, called for immediate intervention to safeguard the transparency and fairness of the counting process. Additionally, alarming reports surfaced from several polling stations in Fatehpur Sikri, where the EVMs malfunctioned, disrupting the voting process. We pressed the ECI to instruct its officials to promptly resolve these technical issues and ensure that the counting proceeded smoothly and in strict accordance with the law.

Staying Engaged without Getting Enraged

Besides the legal reconnaissance team, our National War Room also had its own legal team. It was formed towards the end of 2023 during deliberations about the upcoming 2024 elections, with a clear mission to provide the party with strong legal backing. It was tasked with ensuring compliance for all candidates, addressing violations, countering fake and hate news, and monitoring biased reporting.

Nishant Mandal, an accomplished lawyer with a deep understanding of electoral law, headed the team. He took charge of coordinating the legal strategies across multiple states. His leadership proved invaluable as the team faced numerous challenges, from ensuring candidate compliance to addressing last-minute legal hurdles.

Once the legal unit was established, it became clear that it

Hindustan Times, 4 June 2024, https://tinyurl.com/mr3tnm7s. Accessed on 27 December 2024.

[34]Sheoran, Abhishek, 'Congress To Move Court Over Alleged Fraud In Vote Counting In Six Seats Of UP, Salman Khurshid To Fight Legal Battle', *Jagran English*, 10 June 2024, https://tinyurl.com/44jaj4ku. Accessed on 27 December 2024.

needed to focus on key areas such as legal compliance, identifying propaganda and countering biased media. Upholding Gandhian principles of non-violence and truth was essential, reflecting the core values of the Congress party. Despite unfair practices by investigative agencies, media and institutions, the legal team was committed to lawful, peaceful methods of countering their opponents' tactics.

The unit was designed to operate on a national scale, bringing together seasoned lawyers and energetic, young minds to handle the complexities of election laws. Sasikanth Senthil, using his vast administrative experience, coordinated with each state to understand the unique challenges faced by their legal teams. Advocate Mohammed Ali Khan played a crucial role in coordinating with the ECI, filing petitions in courts, and assisting in all legal matters related to the party's activities.

When the ECI held a press conference in mid-March to announce the schedule for the general elections, the legal team was ready to act. The election, the second longest in Indian history, was spread across seven phases over six weeks, requiring constant vigilance and coordination from the legal unit.

As the election dates neared, the legal team held meetings with the media and communications teams to ensure everyone was prepared. They focused on three key areas: the candidates, the organization, and the ground-level party workers.

The legal team meticulously handled the nominations of the candidates, ensuring that all documents were prepared with great care. Despite attempts by opponents to block the nominations, no Congress candidate faced any issues during the scrutiny, except for one in Indore who withdrew unexpectedly.[35] This incident was a blow to the party, but the legal team continued its work unshaken.

---

[35] Mohan J., Anand, 'After Surat, another jolt to Congress as its Indore candidate withdraws nomination', *The Indian Express*, 30 April 2024, https://tinyurl.com/5n6tztt2. Accessed on 27 December 2024.

Throughout the campaign, the legal team monitored compliance, trained stakeholders, and resolved issues as they arose, often working around the clock. Congress candidates in BJP-ruled states faced difficulties in securing permissions for rallies and helicopter landings, as well as baseless accusations regarding campaign expenditures. The legal team defended the party's rights, addressing these challenges with determination. It used the ECI's Suvidha App to streamline permissions and promptly addressed delays or glitches by working closely with returning officers. In BJP-ruled states, vehicles carrying guarantee cards were stopped and notices were issued alleging privacy violations in the distribution. Despite these setbacks, the party's legal team defended its actions before the ECI, respecting the rules while continuing to reach out to the public.

Many complaints were filed about violations of the Model Code of Conduct, particularly hate speech and fake propaganda, but the action was often slow.[36] Despite this, the legal team remained focused on developmental issues, leaving it to the people of India to judge the ruling government's tactics.

The legal team also kept a close watch on media coverage, which often displayed a clear bias against the Congress party. Although the party considered approaching the News Broadcasters and Digital Association, it ultimately chose to focus on immediate concerns, monitoring and responding to social media violations and other issues.

During the first phase of voting on 19 April, the war room and the legal team were on high alert from early morning. They ensured polling agents were properly trained and prepared to

---

[36]Panjiar, Tejasi, and Shravani Nag Lanka, '#FreeAndFair: Late to the Party(s): How ECI dragged its feet in the 2024 General Election', *Internet Freedom Foundation*, 18 June 2024, https://tinyurl.com/2hu866ab. Accessed on 15 January 2025.

handle discrepancies, such as issues with Form 17C.[37] The team also kept a close eye on voter turnout and discrepancies in voter registration, particularly in BJP-ruled states where families of voters were sometimes missing from the rolls.

As the election phases progressed, new challenges arose, including violence in Andhra Pradesh and West Bengal, voter intimidation, and rumours of EVM tampering.[38] [39] [40] The legal team worked tirelessly to resolve these issues, coordinating with ECI observers and ensuring a smooth election process.

Each phase of the election felt like an entire election process, requiring the legal team to manage multiple tasks at once. From filing nominations to training polling agents, the team repeated these tasks in seven phases. The training sessions, led by Senthil, simplified complex legal matters for candidates and agents, ensuring they were well-prepared. Despite the numerous challenges, the legal team maintained a strict policy of adhering to facts and avoided the use of false information or propaganda.

---

[37] A crucial document detailing the votes cast at each polling station provided by the ECI to polling agents.
[38] 'Violence in Bengal, Andhra mars the 4th phase of LS polls', *The Times of India*, 13 May 2024, https://tinyurl.com/3dva95pk. Accessed on 27 December 2024.
[39] 'Election wrap: Bengal sees poll violence; Supriya Sule files complaint with EC over NCP MLA 'threatening' her party worker', *The Indian Express*, https://tinyurl.com/ycxvv2hk. Accessed on 27 December 2024.
[40] Kumar, Abhijeet, 'Political uproar over EVM 'unlocking'; Elon Musk joins debate. Key points', *Business Standard*, 17 June 2024, https://tinyurl.com/y6hss64a. Accessed on 27 December 2024.

SIX

THE MANDATE AND THE MESSAGE

After an in-depth analysis by our war room, we were confident of winning around 110–120 seats. However, the exit poll results on 1 June belied all reports from the field, which had progressively tilted in favour of the INDIA Alliance. All the polls universally gave the BJP a runaway victory. They forecast that the BJP and its allies would win more than 350 seats in the Lok Sabha, prompting Congress leaders to express reservations about the reliability of the projections.

Our alliance partners put up a brave face, and the usual responses about such polls being often unreliable were given out. But there were worries given the recent questions about voter data. However, we found some reassurance in the assessments of seasoned pollsters like Yogendra Yadav,[1] along with independent journalists like Mahesh Choudhary[2] and alternative media outlets,[3] who predicted that the BJP's seat count would be in a more modest range of 220–230.[4] Unverified reports claimed that several exit polls were supposedly moderated under the ruling party's 'advise'.[5] [6] [7] [8]

---

[1] '2024 Lok Sabha Elections: Shekhar Gupta in conversation with Yogendra Yadav', *The Print*, 4 June 2024, https://tinyurl.com/b9tdu8rb. Accessed on 2 December 2024.
[2] 'BJP is fading out in Rajasthan this time? | 2024 ELECTIONS | PM MODI | INDIA ALLIANCE', *Satya Hindi*, 30 March 2024, https://tinyurl.com/52eu4286. Accessed on 2 December 2024.
[3] News Nasha, 'Lok Sabha Election Results 2024: Strong Room', *YouTube*, https://tinyurl.com/2zpdyzzw. Accessed on 15 January 2025.
[4] 'Who will be ahead in 2nd phases poll | LOKSABHA ELECTION 2024', *Satya Hindi*, 21 April 2024, https://tinyurl.com/3a4dxxkd. Accessed on 2 December 2024.
[5] Bhattacharya, Snigdhendu, 'Was There a Scam in India's Exit Poll Predictions?', *The Diplomat*, 12 June 2024, https://tinyurl.com/vv66m335. Accessed on 15 January 2025.
[6] Chakravarty, Praveen, 'The world's first "Exit Poll Stock Market Scam"', *Deccan Herald*, 9 June 2024, https://tinyurl.com/eytpn9n5. Accessed on 15 January 2025.
[7] Balakrishnan, Palan, 'Stock market surge, exit polls, Rahul Gandhi's questions: Who knew what, when?', *The Telegraph*, 7 June 2024, https://tinyurl.com/2h23awtv. Accessed on 15 January 2025.
[8] 'TMC writes to Sebi, demands probe into exit polls for 'manipulating' stock market', *The Times of India*, 6 June 2024, https://tinyurl.com/3dyfh6cb. Accessed on 15 January 2025.

Inevitably, speculation began about an advance coverup for a manipulated result in favour of the government.[9]

Fortunately, all these fears turned out to be unwarranted because it was another story once the results hit the television channels on 4 June. The BJP did not win a majority, but it emerged as the largest single party, winning 240 seats. The BJP-led NDA (with the JD[U] and the TDP, two slippery partners) won 293 seats, enough to be invited to form the government. Within the INDIA bloc, the Congress led with 99 of the 328 seats it contested and became the cutting edge of the alliance. With these numbers, the Congress was all set to claim the position of Leader of Opposition (LoP) in the Lok Sabha.

In retrospect, I wonder how so many pollsters could have been wrong. (See table)[10]

TABLE 2

	NDA	INDIA
India Today, Axis My India Polls	361–401	131–166
C Voter	353–383	152–182
Today's Chanakya	385–415	96–118
CNX	371–401	109–139
Jan Ki Baat	362–392	109–139

---

[9]Communist Party of India (Marxist), *Review of the 18th Lok Sabha Elections – June 2024 CC Report*, 4 July 2024, Accessed on 10 December 2024.
[10]'Lok Sabha election 2024 Exit Poll', *India Today*, https://tinyurl.com/4c8xhh89. Accessed on 9 December 2024.

TABLE 3
Axis My India forecast vs outcome[11]

States	NDA	INDIA	NDA	INDIA
Uttar Pradesh	64–67	8–12	36	43
Andhra Pradesh	21–23	0	25	0
Odisha	18–20	0–1	20	1
Telangana	11–12	4–6	8	8
Maharashtra	28–32	16–20	17	30
West Bengal	26–31	11–14	12	30
Uttarakhand	5	0	5	0
Himachal Pradesh	4	0	4	0
Punjab	2–4	7–9	0	10
Haryana	6–8	2–4	5	5
Rajasthan	16–19	5–7	14	10
Madhya Pradesh	28–29	1	29	0
Chhattisgarh	10–11	1	10	1
Jharkhand	8–10	4–6	9	5
Bihar	29–33	7–10	30	9
Kerala	2–3	17–18	1	19
Karnataka	23–25	3–5	19	9
Tamil Nadu	2–4	33–37	0	39
Gujarat	25–26	0–1	24	2

Following the election results, India's wildly inaccurate exit polls sparked dramatic public apologies from polling companies and

---

[11] Axis My India's 2024 Exit Poll – Report Card & Deep Dive, 7 June 2024, https://tinyurl.com/5x7u5vxr. Accessed on 9 December 2024.

calls for investigation into possible manipulation.[12] These polls had pushed the benchmark equity index to a record high on 3 June, followed by a crash a day later when almost $400 billion (₹3,336,284 crore) in value was wiped off the market. Opposition parties called on the country's stock market regulator and Parliament to investigate polling companies and BJP leaders for possible rigging. Rahul Gandhi insisted that people high up in the BJP had carried out a scam and demanded to know whether these polls were actually carried out, their methodology, and the details of the investors.[13]

Message from the States: Decoding the Results

Rahul Gandhi's tireless campaign in the name of the Constitution and in the face of the threat to reverse reservations, as well as the uncompromising demand for a caste census, ensured that out of the 84 reserved SC seats in the country, we won twenty compared to six in 2019. The BJP's number went down to 30 from 46 in 2019. The INDIA Alliance notably increased its SC vote share, from 28 per cent in the 2019 elections to 46 per cent in 2024.[14]

Muslims constitute 14 per cent of India's population. The Congress saw an increase in its Muslim vote share from 33 per cent to 38 per cent. This five per cent gain reflects the party's

---

[12]'After Lok Sabha exit polls overestimated NDA victory, public apologies and calls for probe follow', *The Economic Times*, 6 June 2024, https://tinyurl.com/mp2axdk3. Accessed on 15 January 2025.
[13]'How India's exit polls got the 2024 Lok Sabha election horribly wrong', *Frontline*, 7 June 2024, https://tinyurl.com/4szva6nm. Accessed on 30 November 2024.
[14]Verma, Lalmani, and Anjishnu Das, 'BJP retains edge in overall victory margin, but Congress wins bigger in SC, ST seats', *The Indian Express*, 11 June 2024, https://tinyurl.com/2dvdrk5v. Accessed on 9 December 2024.

efforts to rebuild trust and reconnect with Muslim voters.[15] Even more striking is the performance of the INDIA Alliance, which saw its Muslim vote percentage surge to 42 per cent, a significant increase from the 19 per cent it secured in 2019.[16] This 23 per cent increase suggests a robust consolidation of Muslim votes towards the INDIA Alliance. Parties that were not part of INDIA or NDA, like the BSP, suffered the most. They lost 22 per cent of the Muslim vote share.

A state-wise analysis of the results will help us understand the bigger picture.

Uttar Pradesh

Uttar Pradesh was the safe haven for the BJP, but that gave in to the united efforts of Rahul Gandhi and Akhilesh Yadav with a 6:37 seat ratio. But this does not tell the whole story. We got less than a fair share of seats, but at the time, no one believed we could make a serious dent in UP.

However, internal reports made it clear that the SP had disappointed the Muslims, and the Dalits remained wary of the Yadav dominance. In these elections, upper-caste votes moved tentatively to the alliance, more where Congress candidates were contesting, less elsewhere.[17] The OBCs were moderately attracted to the alliance, with the Yadav votes consolidating under the Samajwadi Party and not splitting for the BJP as they did in 2019. In the end, a significant chunk of the Dalit vote

---

[15]Kidwai, Rasheed, and Samrat Sharma, 'Are Muslim voters the real game changers of 2024 Lok Sabha elections?', *India Today*, 7 June 2024, https://tinyurl.com/8zj3sk5z. Accessed on 9 December 2024.
[16]Ibid.
[17]Tiwari, Amitabh, 'UP poll debacle report – Why BJP lost non-Yadav OBC and non-Jatav support', *India Today*, 19 June 2024, https://tinyurl.com/krj7edts. Accessed on 15 January 2025.

(Jatav) returned to the alliance after being wooed by Akhilesh's PDA push, but mainly because of Rahul's tireless efforts. It is important to understand this shift in the political landscape of Uttar Pradesh. In this state, OBCs can be categorized into a few broad groups. First, there are the farming OBCs, such as Jats, Gujjars, Yadavs, Kurmis and Shakyas, often landowning and with representation in socialist parties that emerged from the Lohiaite movement. Second are OBCs, such as Sahus, Telis, Kalwars, Chaurasias and Tamolis, associated with trade. Third, OBCs, such as Kumhars, Sonars, Prajapati and Lohars. Fourth, the service-provider OBCs like Nais and Kahars. Fifth, the rivers OBCs, such as Mallahs, Kewats, Binds and Kashyaps. The latter four groups, referred to as Extremely Backward Classes (EBCs), found marginal representation in mainstream political outfits and formed their political fronts, vying for alliances with larger parties.[18][19][20][21] These OBC communities comprise more than thirty per cent of the state's population, with Yadavs accounting for another twelve per cent.[22]

The BJP had reached out to these OBCs in response to the dominant Yadavs as they scattered from a declining BSP. But, in

---

[18]Pandey, Sanjay, 'Lok Sabha polls 2024: Parties scramble for OBC votes in Uttar Pradesh', *Deccan Herald*, 13 April 2024, https://tinyurl.com/y4mbe999. Accessed on 15 January 2025.

[19]'UP's Caste Politics Churned By New Other Backward Classes (OBC) Order', *NDTV*, 1 September 2022, https://tinyurl.com/stn9f3hm. Accessed on 15 January 2025.

[20]'The OBCs are emerging as key to success in UP elections', *National Herald*, 21 August 2021, https://tinyurl.com/wrw8hwua. Accessed on 15 January 2025.

[21]'Caste-based Uttar Pradesh parties bargaining hard with major parties for larger slice of poll pie', *The Indian Express*, 25 August 2021, https://tinyurl.com/ye4rae2u. Accessed on 15 January 2025.

[22]Rashid, Omar, 'In Caste-Ridden Uttar Pradesh, is Ghosi By-poll Signal for 2024?', *NewsClick*, 12 September 2023, https://tinyurl.com/3nebv3j2. Accessed on 15 January 2025.

2024, Akhilesh consciously decided to restrict his assertion of the Yadav community to five members of his clan and relied heavily on the EBCs. The Congress campaign fortified this position by hammering the issue of caste census along with the protection of the Constitution.

Then, there were other events too that had a lasting impact. After Akhilesh's visit to the Siddhapeeth Baba Gauri Shankar Mahadev temple in Kannauj during the campaign in May, BJP workers cleaned the temple with *gangajal* (holy water) in an attempt to purify it. The Samajwadi Party leadership immediately reacted, 'The BJP believes that backward, Dalit, deprived and exploited people have no right to worship in a Hindu temple.'[23] On the defensive, the BJP leaders claimed that Yadav was an 'electoral Hindu' and was, of course, entitled to enter the temple, but he had been accompanied by Muslims, requiring the purification ritual.[24] The incident was reminiscent of 2017 when Chief Minister Yogi Adityanath had 'purification rituals' performed at his official residence in Lucknow after the Samajwadi Party's defeat.[25] There were no explanations then, but that was after the election. This time, it happened during the campaign.

The Kannauj incident had a silent but profound impact on the backward-caste voters, not just Yadavs but also the plethora of castes stuck between the BJP's Hindutva claims and the Samajwadi Party's underlining of their backward status in its PDA formulation. For the backward castes, and often for the parties that represent them, elections are seen as a space for

---

[23]'BJP Workers Cleaned Kannauj Temple Premises After Akhilesh Yadav's Visit? SP Leader's Big Claim', *Times Now*, 7 May 2024, https://tinyurl.com/8mkm77tp. Accessed on 30 November 2024.
[24]Ibid.
[25]'Purifying rituals at UP CM bungalow, new home for Yogi Adityanath', *The New Indian Express*, 21 March 2017, https://tinyurl.com/r87mde7t. Accessed on 30 November 2024.

samaan (dignity and self-respect) and only then as one for *rozgar* (employment). In an election that was very much about identity—an issue that liberal, upper-caste sections of the Opposition were reluctant to discuss—the Samajwadi Party's winning campaign highlighted what it really meant to be Hindu for a majority under that umbrella.

In addition to the shift in SC votes towards the INDIA Alliance, yet another significant marker in Uttar Pradesh is the marginalization of the BSP, which gave space to the Bhim Army and the emergence of Chandrasekhar Azad as an electoral leader from Nagina. This constituency with a significant Muslim and SC population presents a unique electoral landscape. With Muslims constituting 43 per cent and SCs 21 per cent of the electorate, Chandrasekhar's party, the Aazad Samaj Party (Kanshi Ram), received 512,552 votes in the elections. However, the BSP managed to secure only 13,272 votes.[26] Meanwhile, the NDA experienced a decline in voter support, dropping from 41 per cent in the last election to 35 per cent in 2024.[27]

Electoral analysis conducted by *The Wire* compounded the striking shift in the state's political landscape. Of the 80 parliamentary seats, a significant number of MPs elected, precisely 34, were OBCs. In comparison, 23 MPs were from UCs, 18 were Dalits, and five were Muslims. This strategic move of fielding more OBC and Dalit candidates enabled the Opposition to overpower the BJP in its quest for social justice.

Almost half of the MPs elected from the Opposition—21 out of 43—belonged to the OBC category. Meanwhile, the 36 MPs elected from the NDA predominantly comprised UCs (15),

---

[26]Election Commission of India, Parliamentary Constituency 5 – Nagina (Uttar Pradesh), https://tinyurl.com/mry9v7x8. Accessed on 30 November 2024.
[27]Gupta, Sharad, 'The churn in the Dalit vote bank', *National Herald*, 30 June 2024, https://tinyurl.com/4c23kfsf. Accessed on 9 December 2024.

followed by OBCs (13) and Dalits (8). The BJP and its allies had nominated 29 candidates from backward castes and 34 from UCs. In contrast, the INDIA bloc, which included the Samajwadi Party contesting 62 seats, fielded diverse candidates—33 OBCs, 22 UCs, 19 Dalits (with two running on general seats), and six Muslims.

Of the 43 seats secured by the INDIA Alliance, 16 were clinched by non-Yadav OBCs. Notably, the five Yadavs who won seats for the Samajwadi Party were the late Mulayam Singh Yadav's family members, including Akhilesh himself, who emerged victorious from Kannauj. The Pasi-Kurmi (P-K) formula proved pivotal, aiding the Opposition in defeating the BJP in parts of central and eastern Uttar Pradesh, regions where these communities are densely populated. Specifically, the Samajwadi Party elected seven MPs from the Kurmi caste, five from the Pasi (Dalit) community, three from the Maurya and Shakya castes, two Nishads, and one each from the Jat, Lodhi and Rajbhar castes. An examination of the BJP's elected MPs revealed that the largest segment (13) consisted of eight Brahmins and five Thakurs. This analysis highlights the nuanced and strategic deployment of caste dynamics by both the Opposition and the BJP, underscoring the evolving political narrative in Uttar Pradesh.[28]

Curiously, once community identity (caste) comes to the fore, it is generally acknowledged and supported as a legitimate claim to political representation. Now, there is of course a finer distinction between OBCs and EBCs. A similar attempt by Muslim groups to create a distinction between general-class Muslims (known as *shurfa*), *pasmanda* (backward), and *ati pasmanda* has not worked. The unity of Muslims is also seen as suspicious and an invitation

---

[28] Rashid, Omar, 'Due to INDIA Bloc's Stellar Show, Backward Caste MPs Outnumber Those from Upper Caste in UP', *The Wire*, 6 June 2024, https://tinyurl.com/a4r7w7jz. Accessed on 30 November 2024.

for polarization.[29] Muslims, on the other hand, express discomfort with being referred to as minorities, a term commonly used to refer to them and other minorities collectively. It was the Sachar Committee that used the term 'Muslims' in a departure from standard practice.[30]

This time, Muslims across the country, particularly in Uttar Pradesh, demonstrated solidarity with Congress and are watching intently for signs of appreciation and political reward.[31] As per a CSDS survey, 92 per cent of Muslims in the state voted for the INDIA Alliance.[32] The Congress had already sensed this shift as we prepared for the elections, realizing in 2019 that the Muslim vote was gravitating towards the Samajwadi Party in the quest to uproot the BJP. Consequently, Congress fell to an all-time low of two per cent and two assembly seats.[33] Rightly or otherwise, the Samajwadi Party had to carry the baggage of a disenchanted Azam Khan and the murder of Atiq Ahmed and his brother. Extrajudicial executions seem to have come to stay in Uttar Pradesh under Chief Minister Yogi Adityanath, targeting certain communities. The macabre predicted killing of fugitive

---

[29]Singh, Rajesh Kumar, 'PM Modi's Pasmanda outreach a step forward, say backward class Muslim leaders', *Hindustan Times*, 29 June 2023, https://tinyurl.com/4uv6k5kb. Accessed on 15 January 2025.

[30]Prime Minister's High Level Committee, *Social, Economic and Educational Status of the Muslim Community of India: A Report*, November 2006, https://tinyurl.com/mu9ncd89. Accessed on 31 December 2024.

[31]Bhattacharya, Snigdhendu, 'How Minorities Voted in the Indian General Election', *The Diplomat*, 10 June 2024, https://tinyurl.com/ycka2mpf. Accessed on 31 December 2024.

[32]Beg, Mirza Asmer, et al., 'CSDS-Lokniti post-poll survey: Why the BJP underperformed in U.P.', *The Hindu*, 8 June 2024, https://tinyurl.com/574hps38. Accessed on 30 November 2024.

[33]Dhingra, Sanya, '"Threat" to Constitution, Dalit-Muslim-OBC alliance — how SP won over Dalits in UP & challenges ahead', *The Print*, 9 June 2024, https://tinyurl.com/4hvyam9b. Accessed on 30 November 2024.

Vikas Dubey and the reluctance of the public to come forward to give evidence before the Commission set up by the Supreme Court is a sad commentary on how the rule of law is treated under the BJP governments.

Clearly, the 'soft Hindutva' thesis must be buried once and for all. Yet, it is fair to admit that a balance between ideology and strategy needs to be maintained periodically, so long as the latter does not overwhelm the former. The fear of appeasement charges must not be countered by avoiding issues dear to Muslims but by an honest projection of the truth. Unity in diversity is the basis of a pluralistic society; social conduct and institutions often differ for different religions and communities. Our national obligation is to understand each other's experiences better and concentrate on the value they add to our collective life, rather than resenting differences per se. The UCC phantom unleashed by the BJP has brought them few dividends so far, mainly because Hinduism and tribal culture do not easily fit into a uniform institutional behaviour. But we may see more of this in the months to come.

For now, though, let me analyze the hits and the misses in my home state. We regained Prayagraj (Allahabad) after 40 years. Ujjwal Raman Singh, son of Rewati Raman Singh and a recent recruit to the Congress, polled 462,145 votes. Earlier, Amitabh Bachchan had won the seat in 1984 against Hemwati Nandan Bahuguna.

Rahul Gandhi won Rae Bareli, a seat former Congress president Sonia Gandhi had vacated when she filed her nomination for the Rajya Sabha seat from Rajasthan in February 2024. His impressive win and decision to opt for Rae Bareli opened up Wayanad in Kerala for Priyanka Gandhi. Now that the by-election has been held, we can look forward to the brother-sister combine creating restless moments on the treasury benches in the Lok Sabha.

In Amethi, Kishori Lal Sharma, affectionately known as 'Kishori Bhaiya', was pitched against union minister Smriti Irani. This was a strategic masterstroke. Sharma has been a loyal member of the Congress party for over four decades, with his political journey beginning in Amethi in 1983 alongside Rajiv Gandhi. Quickly becoming an indispensable figure, Sharma's bond with the Gandhi family strengthened after the tragic death of Rajiv Gandhi in 1991. He emerged as a key player in managing the Amethi and Rae Bareli constituencies, especially during the absence of the Gandhis. Irani's defeat to Sharma by 167,196 votes must have been a shock.[34] Mocking the decades of faithful service of the man who has been a byword for Amethi was a mistake that cost her dearly.

In Saharanpur, Imran Masood secured victory with a substantial margin of 64,542 votes.[35] According to him, past reservations about his sharp attacks on PM Modi had diluted considerably, and a chunk of the Thakur votes went to him.

The seat-sharing Alliance Committee could not deliver Farrukhabad, Bhadohi (Rajesh Mishra, former MP, deserted the party and joined the BJP), Jalaun (for Brijlal Khabri, former UPCC President) and Banda (for Nasimuddin Siddiqui), all of whom were squeezed out by the SP.[36]

Alok Misra of Kanpur lost by a narrow margin of 20,968 votes in a race expected to be a win.[37] Kanpur has historically been a Congress stronghold, with Sriprakash Jaiswal winning three consecutive terms before losing in 2014.

In Fatehpur Sikri, ex-army man Ramnath Singh Sikarwar,

---

[34]Kalita, Bishal, 'Amethi Election Results 2024 Highlights: Kisori Lal defeats Smriti Irani by 167196 votes', *Hindustan Times*, 4 June 2024, https://tinyurl.com/3rf35etk. Accessed on 30 November 2024.
[35]Election Commission of India, https://tinyurl.com/35dkvcpd. Accessed on 30 November 2024.
[36]"Former Congress MP from Varanasi Rajesh Mishra joins BJP', *The Hindu*, 5 March 2024, https://tinyurl.com/3u5hpr5n. Accessed on 31 December 2024.
[37]Election Commission of India, https://tinyurl.com/t9e6aude. Accessed on 30 November 2024.

affectionately known as Fauji Baba, faced a heartbreaking loss by 43,405 votes.[38] Sikarwar, a Kargil War veteran who returned to his village, is revered as the voice of the poor in Fatehpur Sikri. For 20 years, he lived in a temple; his only possessions were a carpet and a bucket in his car. During his campaigns, he adopted a unique approach, placing his bucket in the village centre, seeking funds and support from the people. Despite losing the last election by just one per cent of the votes, Sikarwar persisted in his campaign efforts, travelling by bicycle and relying on the kindness and contributions of the local community.

In Amroha, Kunwar Danish Ali contested but faced defeat by 28,670 votes. The BSP's significant vote count of 164,099 played a crucial role in his loss.[39]

An interesting development took place in my traditional seat of Farrukhabad, which the Samajwadi Party adamantly took in the alliance. In compliance with the alliance obligations, I travelled to Kaimganj, my home in Farrukhabad, for a well-attended public meeting. The event was organized by Maria Alam, the daughter of my late cousin, Izhar Alam. Both father and daughter were longtime Samajwadi Party members, and our relationship was formal. Several leaders of both parties attended the meeting. During her speech, Maria used emphatic phrases, including the need for a 'vote jihad'.[40] There was no reaction from the audience.

Somewhat later, when the media asked me to comment, I said that it should be understood as *sangharsh* (struggle) but that we abjured using words prone to misunderstanding and misuse.

---

[38]Ibid.
[39]Election Commission of India, https://tinyurl.com/535hpm8h. Accessed on 30 November 2024.
[40]PTI, 'Lok Sabha Elections 2024: SP leader Maria Alam's appeal for 'vote jihad' sparks row', *Deccan Herald*, 30 April 2024, https://tinyurl.com/459448yf. Accessed on 30 November 2024.

Yet, that led to an FIR against her and me.[41] Presumably, her because of what she said, and me because I did not say it! Or is it because I have a blood relationship? Here, it is pertinent to highlight a dimension of the ECI's 'level playing field'. Filing such unviable FIRs leads to huge headlines that can be misleading and irreparably damage reputations. And, of course, the real meaning and intent of jihad is obscured.

PM Modi was quick to use it in various speeches, 'INDI Alliance has asked Muslims to go for vote jihad. This has come from an educated family, not from a child coming out of a madrasa. INDI Alliance is saying that all Muslims should get together and vote. The INDI Alliance has insulted democracy and the Constitution.'[42]

Maria was understandably distressed and went into seclusion for days on end, but clarified that a 'vote jihad' was the only way to remove this government. 'People say that the Constitution and democracy are under threat. But I say that *insaniyat* (humanity) is under threat.'[43] Showing a young lady support and courtesy, irrespective of personal relationships, cannot be grounds for an electoral misdemeanour, but one must be extra cautious when election fever makes things volatile.

PM Modi secured victory in the Varanasi constituency with a narrow margin of 152,513 votes.[44] This marks a significant

---

[41] 'FIR lodged against Congress' Salman Khurshid & SP leader Maria Alam Khan for allegedly asking for votes on religious lines', *The Economic Times*, 30 April 2024, https://tinyurl.com/4fv6mtm2. Accessed on 30 November 2024.

[42] 'PM Modi Says UP Leader's "Vote Jihad" Remark Exposed INDIA Bloc Strategy', *NDTV*, 2 May 2024, https://tinyurl.com/ydnn334v. Accessed on 30 November 2024.

[43] Sinha, Sahil, 'Salman Khurshid's niece sparks row with 'vote jihad' appeal, case filed', *India Today*, 30 April 2024, https://tinyurl.com/5ayey57p. Accessed on 30 November 2024.

[44] Election Commission of India, https://tinyurl.com/t9e6aude. Accessed on 30 November 2024.

narrowing compared to his previous margins in the 2019 and 2014 Lok Sabha elections. In the early trends, the leading position of UPCC president Ajay Rai caused concern within the BJP faction.

Arun Govil, known for his portrayal of Lord Ram in the beloved epic *Ramayan*, secured victory in Meerut by a narrow margin of 10,585 votes. It was later discovered that in Meerut 61,365 voters were removed, and more than 100,000 new voters were added to the electoral rolls before the BJP's Arun Govil emerged victorious over the Samajwadi Party's Sunita Verma.[45] BSP's Devvrat Kumar Tyagi got 87,025 votes and helped secure Govil his seat.[46] In 1988, Govil supported the Congress party in Allahabad during the campaign for Sunil Shastri, who contested against V.P. Singh. Govil appeared at the request of former prime minister Rajiv Gandhi. Despite his efforts, the Congress party failed to win the seat.

However, it was Ayodhya that took the cake, where the refrain of *Na Mathura, Na Kashi, Abki Baar Awadhesh Pasi* drove the Samajwadi Party candidate, Awadhesh Prasad, to a stunning victory. The message was clear: Don't mess with people's rights in the name of *Maryada Purushottam*. Learn to honour the avowed precepts of Ram Rajya. All that BJP spokesperson Sudhanshu Trivedi could say was that in gloating over seats associated with the story of Ramji, the Congress party was forced to concede that Ram existed.[47] He needs to be reminded that Congress has never questioned, and will never question, Ram, but we remain rooted

---

[45] Mittal, Sumedha, 'BJP won Meerut with thin margin. Its 2 booths have 27% fake voters', *Newslaundry*, 24 December 2024, https://tinyurl.com/2rrvkjrj. Accessed on 15 January 2025.

[46] Election Commission of India, https://tinyurl.com/3dnmvkwf. Accessed on 30 November 2024.

[47] ANI News, '"Jo Log Khte The Ram Ki Saboot Do…" Sudhanshu Trivedi reacts on BJP's Ayodhya loss, slams INDIA bloc', *YouTube*, https://tinyurl.com/y5pw2z9c. Accessed on 15 January 2025.

in our opinion that obeisance to Ram should not be reduced to a political slogan.

In my opinion, the statement of Lallu Singh, the BJP MP candidate from Faizabad, regarding the formation of government and changing the Constitution appears to have had unintended consequences for the BJP. He insisted that 'the government can be formed with 272 MPs, but to amend the Constitution or create a new one, we need more than a two-thirds majority (in the 2024 Lok Sabha polls).'[48]

Despite the party's ambitions and efforts on its Ram Van Gaman Path project, the BJP lost all the seats along this stretch that figure in the history of Lord Ram. The party faced defeats in five out of nine seats in the Ayodhya region. These included Sultanpur, where SP candidate Rambhual Nishad defeated BJP's Maneka Gandhi, and Basti, where SP's Ram Prasad Chaudhary defeated BJP's incumbent MP Harish Dwivedi. Additionally, the BJP also lost in Ambedkar Nagar and Shrawasti, as it did in 2019. In Ambedkar Nagar, SP's Lalji Verma defeated BJP's Ritesh Pandey. In Shrawasti, SP's Ram Shiromani Verma secured victory over BJP's Saket Misra by more than 76,000 votes.[49] Saket is the son of Nripendra Misra, the Ram Temple construction committee chairman. The BJP suffered further setbacks losing nine out of twelve seats in the Varanasi region, which includes Chandauli, Robertsganj, Ghazipur, Ghosi, Lalganj, Jaunpur, Machhlishahr, Azamgarh and Ballia.

After the election results, Akhilesh claimed the end of communal politics in UP.[50] That might be a premature obituary,

---

[48]'Faizabad MP pitches for new Constitution', *Hindustan Times*, 15 April 2024, https://tinyurl.com/2zthuvfh. Accessed on 30 November 2024.
[49]Election Commission of India, https://tinyurl.com/t9e6aude. Accessed on 30 November 2024.
[50]'Lok Sabha polls marked end of communal politics in India, says Akhilesh', *Business Standard*, 2 July 2024, https://tinyurl.com/4ps73a58. Accessed on 31 December 2024.

but it is clear that polarization has limits in our society. The BJP myth that India had changed irreversibly has been busted.

Even though commentators might read more into the results in Uttar Pradesh than is justified, the results cannot be seen as a conclusive rejection of Hindu majoritarianism, or as an answer to rising poverty or unemployment. A post-election survey by the CSDS showed overwhelming support for BJP's inauguration of the Ram Temple.[51] It also showed no precipitous loss of support for the BJP among the poor. While the party lost three percentage points among upper- and middle-income groups, it lost only one point among the lower-income groups and gained one point among the poor. Over the past five years, rising inequality, deaths during the COVID-19 pandemic, and neglect of migrant workers in the aftermath affected the poor severely, yet failed to become major issues despite the Opposition's attempts to articulate them. Surprisingly, the Ram Temple did not rise to be a major driving issue for the BJP.

While we celebrate the derailing of the two-engine sarkar in Uttar Pradesh, we have a major task on our hands in terms of the way ahead to the 2027 assembly elections. Despite the resurgence of Congress, our seat footprint is modest and might not fructify into a viable number of seats to contest. That would upset the balance of power and prospects.

Rajasthan

We went into the election somewhat upbeat despite failing to form government in the assembly. The Sachin Pilot issue dragged the assembly elections despite formal statements of peace from Chief Minister Ashok Gehlot and Pilot himself. People believe that we could have gotten us through with a little extra effort. Fortunately,

---

[51] Social and Political Barometer Postpoll Study 2024-Survey Findings, Lokniti, CSDS, https://tinyurl.com/53u2ccrd. Accessed on 9 December 2024.

interpersonal communication was much better for the general elections, and the results are there for everyone to see. Though we drew a blank in the last parliamentary election, this time we could restrict the BJP to fourteen. We got eight seats, a few less than expected.[52] In a significant electoral outcome, the BJP faced defeat in Banswara, a constituency where PM Modi had stirred controversy with remarks about Muslims.[53] Bharat Adivasi Party (BAP) won the seat. We had an informal understanding with the BAP, although no formal alliance was in place between the two parties.

Haryana

The seats in the state were caught in the logjam competition between the camps of Bhupinder Singh Hooda and Kumari Selja. The simmering was apparent long before the elections as parallel road shows projected respective strengths. Deepak Babaria, the party in-charge, Madhusudan Mistry, and I were tasked with finding common ground between the two groups. Randeep Surjewala and Kumari Selja, both general secretaries of the party, were digging in for Shruti Choudhry from Bhiwani-Mahendragarh, but our best efforts failed and we lost the seat. Kiran Choudhry and daughter Shruti resigned from the party and joined the BJP. Our experiment with Raj Babbar in Gurugram failed, possibly because of paucity of time. Ultimately, we won five seats—Sirsa, Sonipat, Ambala, Rohtak and Hisar.[54]

---

[52]Election Commission of India, https://tinyurl.com/32eykxpr. Accessed on 2 December 2024.
[53]'BJP loses in Rajasthan's Banswara, where PM Modi made hate speech against Muslims', *The News Minute*, 5 June 2024, https://tinyurl.com/bdfa25py. Accessed on 31 December 2024.
[54]Srinivasan, Chandrashekar, 'Ahead Of Poll, BJP Now Has Members From Haryana's 3 Big Political Families', *NDTV*, 19 June 2024, https://tinyurl.com/y6k8fjey. Accessed on 31 December 2024.

Bihar

The Mahagathbandhan, led by the RJD, faced a critical challenge with the inclusion of Rajesh Ranjan alias Pappu Yadav, who merged his Jan Adhikar Party (Loktantrik) with the Congress and asserted his claim to the Purnia Lok Sabha seat in North Bihar.[55] Despite Akhilesh Prasad Singh (a Bhumihar) being BPCC president, he could not garner upper-caste votes, not even for his son. In contrast, Pappu Yadav won Purnia by a margin of 23,847 votes, despite the RJD denying him the ticket first and then campaigning against him.[56] Bima Bharti of the RJD got 27,120 votes.[57]

The Congress contested nine seats, and the RJD contested 23 seats. We won three seats—Kishanganj, Katihar and Sasaram—and RJD won four.[58] In Bihar, a lot of work is needed on the drawing board and, thereafter, on the ground. Prashant Kishor is lurking on the side to enter once he spots a gap.

Delhi

The BJP triumphed in the capital for the third consecutive time, securing all seven Lok Sabha seats. Current trends indicate the

---

[55] Bhelari, Amit, 'Pappu Yadav to fight from Purnea LS seat, file nomination on April 4', *The Hindu*, 2 April 2024, https://tinyurl.com/2s4zmsw7. Accessed on 31 December 2024.

[56] General Election to Parliamentary Constituencies: Trends & Results June-2024 Winning Candidate - Independent (Bihar), Election Commission of India, https://tinyurl.com/5n7y8hem. Accessed on 2 December 2024.

[57] General Election to Parliamentary Constituencies: Trends & Results June-2024 Parliamentary Constituency 12–Purnia (Bihar), https://tinyurl.com/5n7n5b8k. Accessed on 2 December 2024.

[58] General Election to Parliamentary Constituencies: Trends & Results June-2024 Bihar (Total PC–40), https://tinyurl.com/2nz2h6nj. Accessed on 2 December 2024.

following vote shares: BJP at 54 per cent, AAP at 24 per cent, and Congress at 19 per cent.[59] Unlike other states where we rivalled the regional party, in Delhi, the workers failed to overcome the differences in working style and perhaps more. J.P. Agarwal, a favourite from Chandni Chowk, lost to the BJP, as did Kanhaiya Kumar from Northeast Delhi. Both had surpassed Sandeep Dikshit, who entered the race somewhat late and could not pick one over the other of the two seats.

Madhya Pradesh

The BJP won all 29 seats. The Indore seat had NOTA 218674 because Congress candidate Akshay Bam had favoured the BJP.[60] Former chief minister Shivraj Singh Chouhan found himself in a spectacular personal electoral result, winning in Vidisha by over eight lakh votes.[61] For us, the transition to a new leadership in Madhya Pradesh after the assembly elections does not seem to have settled. Kamal Nath's unique, forceful, perhaps eccentric style of politics seems to have been overtaken by the changing times. Kamal Nath's son, Nakul Nath, lost the family bastion of Chhindwara. The unimaginable had happened. Unfortunately, Digvijaya Singh failed to recapture his political kingdom.

---

[59]General Election to Parliamentary Constituencies: Trends & Results June-2024 NCT OF Delhi (Total PC - 7), Election Commission of India, https://tinyurl.com/yc3xkrdr. Accessed on 9 December 2024.

[60]General Election to Parliamentary Constituencies: Trends & Results June-2024 Parliamentary Constituency 26 – INDORE (Madhya Pradesh), Election Commission of India, https://tinyurl.com/yc6kn69y. Accessed on 2 December 2024.

[61]General Election to Parliamentary Constituencies: Trends & Results June-2024 Parliamentary Constituency 18 - VIDISHA (Madhya Pradesh), Election Commission of India, https://tinyurl.com/3y3x9ppr. Accessed on 2 December 2024.

Going forward, we must pick up the pieces and weld them together.

Chhattisgarh

In the aftermath of his defeat in the 2023 assembly elections, former chief minister Bhupesh Baghel pinned his hopes on the Lok Sabha election for a chance at redemption. Contesting fiercely from Rajnandgaon against incumbent BJP leader Santosh Pandey, Baghel's campaign aimed to overturn his previous loss but fell short by 44,411 votes.[62] Amidst this electoral setback, the Congress found solace in Jyotsna Charandas Mahant's victory in Korba. Analyzing the electoral dynamics further reveals critical shifts in voter behaviour. In the 2023 assembly elections, the BJP secured 46.27 per cent of the votes, narrowly surpassing Congress's 42.23 per cent.[63] Regional parties and independents together garnered ten per cent of the votes. However, the Lok Sabha election saw a notable change, with the BJP strengthening its hold significantly to capture 52.65 per cent of the vote share. In contrast, the Congress maintained a relatively stable vote share at 41.06 per cent, showing only a marginal decline despite its efforts. The share of regional parties and independents fell to five per cent, suggesting a consolidation of non-BJP votes towards the BJP.[64]

---

[62]General Election to Parliamentary Constituencies: Trends & Results June-2024 Parliamentary Constituency 6 - RAJNANDGAON (Chhattisgarh), Election Commission of India, https://tinyurl.com/ywcpystm. Accessed on 2 December 2024.

[63]General Election to Assembly Constituencies: Trends & Results Dec-2023 – Chhattisgarh, Election Commission of India, https://tinyurl.com/27kysrdf. Accessed on 9 December 2024.

[64]General Election to Parliamentary Constituencies: Trends & Results June-2024 – Chhattisgarh (Total PC - 11), Election Commission of India, https://tinyurl.com/4a8hf4fy. Accessed on 9 December 2024.

Himachal Pradesh

We suffered setbacks because the BJP had poached in the Rajya Sabha elections.[65] Deft handling and walking on the edge just about saved the government. In the following weeks and months, Chief Minister Sukhvinder Singh Sukhu clawed back his majority with triumphant by-election victories.

Odisha

Odisha surprised everyone with the unseating of Naveen Patnaik and the BJP stepping in to fill the vacuum after decades of BJD dominance. Clearly, the voters were irked by the conduct of the all-powerful former CM's close aide, V.K. Pandian, and decided to pack him off—lock, stock and barrel. Shockingly, the Congress leaders did very poorly, but Koraput emerged as a saving grace. The tribal community of Koraput once again rallied behind Saptagiri Sankar Ulaka, carrying a strong sense of pride and purpose. Saptagiri Sankar defeated Kausalya Hikaka of BJD with an impressive margin of 147,744 votes.[66] Ulaka, a young, dynamic leader, had inherited the political legacy of his father, Rama Chandra Ulaka, who was a respected Congress figure with deep roots in the region. As he claimed victory for the fourth time for his family in the Koraput constituency—twice now in his name—the community saw him as more than a politician. He represented the continuity of their aspirations, someone who understood their values and carried forward their collective hope.

---

[65] 'Amid cross-voting, BJP wins 8 UP seats, SP gets 2; Congress loses Himachal seat', *The Indian Express*, 7 April 2024, https://tinyurl.com/4k48xea2. Accessed on 15 January 2025.

[66] 'INC's Saptagiri Shankar defeats BJD's Kausalya Hikaka by 1,47,744 votes', *The Times of India*, 5 June 2024, https://tinyurl.com/mv3azdn9. Accessed on 15 January 2025.

Saptagiri Ulaka's remarkable victory serves as a reminder that perseverance, dedication, and sincerity in public service can still triumph in the realm of politics. As he navigated the intricate landscape of political leadership, he remained focused on a singular goal—to uplift the tribal community, honour their values, and guide them toward a future where tradition and progress could coexist.

Mohammed Moquim's daughter, Sofia Firdous, won his Barabati-Cuttack seat in the Odisha assembly election on her debut. She became the first Muslim woman to win an MLA seat in Odisha, defeating BJP's Purna Chandra Mahapatra by a decisive margin of 8,001 votes. Firdous garnered an impressive 53,339 votes, while Mahapatra trailed with 45,338.[67]

Punjab

Punjab politics seems to have changed dramatically, but not entirely, with the victory of pro-Khalistani leaders Amritpal Singh and Sarabjeet Singh Khalsa keeping the flame of extremism burning.[68] Congress won seven seats, the AAP won three seats, and the SAD won one seat.[69] The decision to steer clear of an alliance for Parliament served us well, although it was mutual. But of course, it would have helped if SAD and BJP had not come together. Former CM Charanjit Singh Channi won the Jalandhar

---

[67]'Meet Sofia Firdous, first Muslim woman to win assembly election in Odisha', *Hindustan Times*, 9 June 2024, https://tinyurl.com/2h828jhv. Accessed on 15 January 2025.

[68]Sehgal, Manjeet, 'How poll win of Khalistan sympathisers in Punjab is both a message and warning', *India Today*, 6 June 2024, https://tinyurl.com/yeynkkm4. Accessed on 31 December 2024.

[69]General Election to Parliamentary Constituencies: Trends & Results June-2024 Punjab (Total PC - 13), Election Commission of India, https://tinyurl.com/23z8xdu7. Accessed on 2 December 2024.

seat. We recaptured Chandigarh, although Manish Tewari replaced Pawan Kumar Bansal. During negotiations with the AAP, we had a difficult time refusing to compromise on Chandigarh while they were determined to retain the seat. The AAP was even inclined to let Bansal contest on their symbol. Naturally, we rejected this idea. However, as it turned out, the party chose to field Manish. Of all the takeaways from the INDIA Alliance, the least we may have got was with AAP. It might have made a similar assessment, quickly indicating the end of the alliance for Delhi.

Maharashtra

Ashok Chavan, Milind Deora and Baba Siddique left the Congress as the elections approached. Then Sanjay Nirupam, the unpredictable firebrand, quit the party over seat-sharing arrangements with the Shiv Sena. The Sena announced candidates for four seats in Mumbai to break the stalemate and continued to protest our decision to contest in Sangli. Although Shiv Sena's Uddhav Thackeray and NCP's Sharad Pawar had the benefit of worker sympathy, the Congress's strike rate was ultimately better, giving it the most seats. The Congress emerged as the largest party by winning thirteen out of seventeen contested seats, accounting for 16.9 per cent of the total seats. Following closely behind, Shiv Sena (Uddhav Balasaheb Thackeray) secured nine out of 21 seats, while the Nationalist Congress Party (Sharadchandra Pawar) won eight seats. In contrast, the BJP won nine out of 28 contested seats, Shiv Sena (under Eknath Shinde) got seven out of 15 seats, and the NCP (under Ajit Pawar) managed to secure only one out of four seats.[70] Understandably, fresh churning began and talks

---

[70] General Election to Parliamentary Constituencies: Trends & Results June-2024 Maharashtra (Total PC - 48), Election Commission of India, https://tinyurl.com/3uc5e7ry. Accessed on 2 December 2024.

of *ghar wapsi* (homecoming) were common. Sharad Pawar gave credence to this by saying people were welcome to return, but obviously under strict conditions.[71][72]

Kerala

The INDIA coalition secured 19 seats, leaving the BJP with just one seat. The Indian Union Muslim League (IUML) maintained their previous tally of two seats. Suresh Gopi of the BJP made history by winning a Lok Sabha seat in Thrissur, marking the party's first victory in the southern state. In Thiruvananthapuram, Rajeev Chandrasekhar of the BJP conceded defeat to Shashi Tharoor, who won by a narrow margin of 16,077 votes, his third consecutive victory.[73]

Telangana

After ruling the state for six months, the Congress faced a crucial test, emerging victorious in eight seats, notably in southern Telangana. These include Peddapalle, Zahirabad, Nagarkurnool, Nalgonda, Bhongir, Warangal, Mahabubabad and Khammam seats with significant margins.[74] The staunch

---

[71]"Pawar Sr on taking back NCP leaders: No issue in welcoming people but conditions apply', *Deccan Herald*, 25 June 2024, https://tinyurl.com/224yemac. Accessed on 15 January 2025.
[72]Marpakwar, Prafulla, 'Door open for legislators to return, hints Sharad Pawar', *The Times of India*, 26 June 2024, https://tinyurl.com/yff6fzfa. Accessed on 15 January 2025.
[73]General Election to Parliamentary Constituencies: Trends & Results June-2024 Parliamentary Constituency 20 - Thiruvananthapuram (Kerala), Election Commission of India, https://tinyurl.com/mtb4hjn7. Accessed on 2 December 2024.
[74]General Election to Parliamentary Constituencies: Trends & Results June-2024, Winning Candidate - Indian National Congress (Telangana), https://tinyurl.com/bvpcmhz9. Accessed on 31 December 2024.

Bharat Rashtra Samiti (BRS) voter base traditionally leans anti-Congress, particularly those involved in the Telangana agitation. Allegations surfaced suggesting that the BRS may have supported the saffron party in exchange for favours, such as facilitating the bail of K. Kavitha, daughter of K. Chandrasekhar Rao.[75] Chief Minister Revanth Reddy argued that compromising BRS interests aimed to appease the BJP would weaken the Congress. Adding weight to this theory, Hyderabad MP-elect Asaduddin Owaisi, formerly allied with KCR, echoed similar sentiments post-election, pointing to instances where BRS leaders and supporters openly backed the BJP.[76] Although writing off a political force is never advisable, prima facie BRS appears in a spiral of free fall with several MLCs and important Rajya Sabha MPs switching to Congress.

Karnataka

The assembly results were refreshing and indeed gave a feeling of a turnaround in the fortunes of the Congress. But it remained a touch-and-go issue until the end. The scales tipped in our favour, but simmering tensions caused by the ambitions of top leaders lingered in the form of speculation on whether the tenure of the CM's post was to be shared. The Lingayats-Vokkaligas alliance, which former prime minister H.D. Deve Gowda had revived for the parliamentary elections, trimmed our victory.

---

[75]'Congress alleges BRS-BJP nexus got bail for Kavitha', *The Hindu*, 27 August 2024, https://tinyurl.com/5n84brft. Accessed on 31 December 2024.
[76]Tomar, Ajay, 'Owaisi wonders whether BRS will merge with BJP, cites media reports', *The New Indian Express*, 17 July 2024, https://tinyurl.com/35s857by. Accessed on 31 December 2024.

West Bengal

Although Mamata Banerjee was an early supporter of the idea of the INDIA Alliance, she was uncomfortable with the thought of a partnership with the Left. Adhir Ranjan Chowdhury, five-time MP and constant detractor of the chief minister, was defeated in Baharampur by the strategically fielded Yusuf Pathan of the TMC. Isha Khan Choudhury became the lone Congress MP from Maldaha Dakshin.

The Northeastern States

Assam: Three seats were won handsomely by Rakibul Hussain, Pradyut Bordoloi and Gaurav Gogoi. We could have won a few more seats if the delimitation had not worked to our disadvantage. Himanta Biswa Sarma's virulent attacks on the *miyan*s, such as bringing up the child marriage issue, may have worked both ways.[77] However, Rakibul Hussain's victory by ten lakh votes against Maulana Badruddin Ajmal finally settled the controversial alliance debate within the party.[78] In the 2021 assembly elections, the Congress lost out in upper Assam and benefited only marginally in the Barak Valley because of the alliance. Our workers' opinion ranged from the need for alliance to the desirability of undeclared cooperation. There are issues about the last delimitation, undertaken by the ECI and not the Delimitation Commission, whose term and mandate had

---

[77] Dutta, Sharangee, 'No polygamy, child marriage: Himanta Sarma's 'conditions' for Bangladeshi Muslims', *India Today*, 24 March 2024, https://tinyurl.com/2c9dppjs. Accessed on 31 December 2024.

[78] General Election to Parliamentary Constituencies: Trends & Results June-2024 Parliamentary Constituency 2 - Dhubri (Assam), Election Commission of India, https://tinyurl.com/49dtmx9x. Accessed on 2 December 2024.

expired.[79] The matter remains pending in the Supreme Court. Many people feel that the delimitation exercise squeezed minorities into limited constituencies, limiting their impact on other areas.[80] [81] [82]

Meghalaya: Congress won one seat. Saleng A. Sangma from Tura breached the monopoly of CM Conrad Sangma in this region. However, Vincent Pala, former central minister and PCC president, lost his traditional seat of Shillong. The sense is that the artificial arrangement with the BJP has reached its sell-by date.

Tripura: Pradyot Bikram Manikya Deb Barma, former acting PCC president who formed his party, TIPRA Motha, allied with the BJP, ensuring that BJP won both the seats.

Manipur: Manipur is a mosaic of diverse ethnic groups, including the Meiteis, Nagas and Chin-Kuki-Mizo tribes. The Meiteis, predominantly Hindus, reside in the Imphal Valley, while the predominantly Christian Nagas and Kukis inhabit the surrounding hills. The strife between Meiteis and Kukis erupted violently on 3 May 2023, and the consequences were devastating. The mobs razed villages, displacing over 60,000 people from their homes. More than 200 individuals lost their lives in the clashes between

---

[79]'AICC forms a panel to delve deep into constituency delimitation exercise in Assam', *The Sentinel*, 13 December 2024, https://tinyurl.com/3f793k69. Accessed on 15 January 2025.

[80]Baruah, Sukrita, 'Discontent over Assam delimitation spreads: Minority, indigenous outfits to sitting MLAs', *The Indian Express*, https://tinyurl.com/yuazdrz5. Accessed on 15 January 2025.

[81]Zaman, Rokibuz, 'Why redrawn electoral boundaries in Assam have confirmed Muslim legislators' worst fears', *Scroll.in*, https://tinyurl.com/2p9sjuzf. Accessed on 15 January 2025.

[82]Baruah, Sukrita, '"We feel we have been divided on basis of religion": In Assam, a delimitation exercise raises questions', *The Indian Express*, https://tinyurl.com/2afx7hyx. Accessed on 15 January 2025.

the majority of Meiteis and the Kukis.[83] The crisis garnered international attention when a harrowing video surfaced showing a mob sexually assaulting two women, casting a stark light on the deepening conflict in Manipur.[84]

The immediate trigger for the violence was a recommendation by the Manipur High Court to include the Meiteis in the ST category. This proposal ignited fears among the Kukis, who worried that such a change would lead to a loss of land and jobs due to potential competition from the Meitei community. Their apprehensions were heightened by the prospect of the Meitei purchasing land in the hills, which had been the exclusive domain of the Kukis.[85]

The state government's plan to identify and evict illegal immigrants from the hills further fuelled tensions.[86] The Kukis were particularly uneasy about the BJP government's proposal to introduce the National Register of Citizens (NRC) and Chief Minister N. Biren Singh's plans to oust illegal immigrants, fearing these actions would disproportionately impact the tribal population.[87]

Although the Meitei comprise 51 per cent of Manipur's

---

[83] 'How Manipur has bled for 19 months with over 200 people killed, 60,000 displaced and counting', *The Telegraph*, 13 November 2024, https://tinyurl.com/6zmwxrch. Accessed on 31 December 2024.

[84] Arya, Divya, 'Manipur assault video emboldens women to speak out', *BBC*, 23 July 2023, https://tinyurl.com/7r5v5c46. Accessed on 31 December 2024.

[85] 'Manipur violence: Who are Meiteis and Kukis? What are they fighting over?', *The Economic Times*, 9 May 2023, https://tinyurl.com/3vh46th6. Accessed on 31 December 2024.

[86] '2,480 illegal immigrants detected in Manipur in 2023 before outbreak of violence: CM', *The Economic Times*, 12 May 2024, https://tinyurl.com/mt6armka. Accessed on 31 December 2024.

[87] Levion, Jimmy, 'Kukis among those worried as Manipur Assembly nod to NRC stirs complex waters', *The Indian Express*, 12 August 2022, https://tinyurl.com/mr3ap8dx. Accessed on 31 December 2024.

population, they own only ten per cent of the land, while the Kukis and Nagas, who make up 40 per cent of the population, occupy 90 per cent of the land. This political landscape, in which the Meitei have been chief ministers since the late 1990s, exacerbated the Kukis' feelings of marginalization and underrepresentation. The state's budget and development initiatives were perceived to be disproportionately focused on the Meitei-dominated Imphal Valley.[88] [89]

Allegations of illegal migration and demographic shifts further strained relations. The higher population growth rate in the hills compared to the valley, as recorded in the 2011 census, fuelled suspicions that people were migrating illegally from neighbouring countries such as Myanmar, Nepal and Bangladesh. These demographic changes heightened the Meiteis' fears of marginalization in their state.

Manipur's proximity to conflict-ridden Myanmar, notorious for poppy cultivation and drug trafficking, added another layer of complexity. Poppy cultivation in the hills of Manipur supported the drug trade and provided a crucial source of livelihood for the tribal groups. The Kukis saw the state government's aggressive war on drugs as an attempt to deprive them of their economic sustenance.

The slow response of the BJP governments in New Delhi and Imphal exacerbated the situation. Despite a complaint being filed immediately after the gang rape of two Kuki women by a Meitei mob in early May, it took the police 78 days to detain the

---

[88] Rathore, Shruti, 'Navigating the Kuki-Meitei Conflict in India's Manipur State', *The Diplomat*, 1 August 2023, https://tinyurl.com/axuapxjy. Accessed on 2 December 2024.

[89] Roy, Esha, 'Manipur's ethnic faultlines: Kuki-Meitei divide & recent unrest', *The Indian Express*, 7 May 2023, https://tinyurl.com/yc87akpv. Accessed on 31 December 2024.

accused.[90] Chief Minister Biren Singh showed extreme reluctance to act against the mobs, further inflaming tensions.[91]

The central government's response was equally troubling. PM Modi remained silent on the Manipur crisis for months, issuing a bland statement only after former Chief Justice of India D.Y. Chandrachud urged the government to act. This delay in addressing the violence solidified the Kuki-Meitei divide, making reconciliation a long and arduous process.

Allegations that the security forces and law enforcement agencies were divided along ethnic lines complicated the situation. If true, these divisions within the institutions meant to maintain order made the volatile environment in Manipur even more difficult to manage.[92]

The Congress won both seats in the traumatized state. Rahul Gandhi was the first leader from Delhi to visit Manipur.[93] The impact of the Bharat Jodo NYAY Yatra and Rahul's message of peace and harmony prevailed in the state. Notably, Rahul kept the focus on Manipur during the Lok Sabha debates, taking the earliest opportunity to visit the troubled state—his third important visit.

---

[90] Rathore, Shruti, 'Navigating the Kuki-Meitei Conflict in India's Manipur State', *The Diplomat*, 1 August 2023, https://tinyurl.com/axuapxjy. Accessed on 2 December 2024.

[91] 'Manipur gang rape: State had not granted sanction to prosecute under sections of promoting enmity, says CBI chargesheet', *The Hindu*, 1 May 2024, https://tinyurl.com/5ar4h8w6. Accessed on 31 December 2024.

[92] Dutta, Srishti B., 'Manipur Violence: Several Organisations Seek President's Rule Citing Biases In Administration', *Indiatimes*, 23 June 2023, https://tinyurl.com/2ewfn6n3. Accessed on 9 December 2024.

[93] 'Congress leader Rahul Gandhi arrives in Imphal on two-day visit to violence-hit Manipur, to visit relief camps', *Financial Express*, 29 June 2023, https://tinyurl.com/3p27vetw. Accessed on 15 January 2025.

Shifts and Continuities

The above analysis is incomplete without a phase-wise comparison of the performance of the Congress and the BJP in 2019 and 2024. The chart below shows an interesting trend over the seven phases. Although the BJP's decline became apparent in the beginning, it was really the third and fourth phases that drove the Congress's revival.

TABLE 4

Phase-wise comparison of BJP's and INC's performance in 2019 and 2024

Phases	2019	2024
1	40	30
	15	27
2	52	47
	18	23
3	72	58
	4	15
4	42	39
	6	14
5	42	39
	1	4
6	40	39
	0	6
7	25	17
	8	9

It appeared that the election was deliberately spread over two months, seemingly to allow PM Modi the opportunity to address the maximum number of rallies across the country. In retrospect, though, it might be said that prolonging the campaign sapped the advantage the BJP might have started with.

Despite this, we are in a unique situation, with PM Modi claiming victory because he is in government for the third consecutive term, albeit in an alliance with the NDA partners, and the INDIA Alliance claiming victory in reducing the BJP to being the single largest party at the mercy of its partners.

For now, the alliance politics seems to be here to stay. The Modi-led BJP government is in a precarious balance with two allies who could easily find a reason to withdraw their support. There are already some inherent contradictions on minority issues, such as UCC and CAA, that could easily blow up.[94] [95] The budget and special status is another trap. There is clearly insufficient data to show that alliances are adequately understood. No one has really worked on the science involved, and most parties make do with ad hoc measures. The JD(U)-RJD saga in Bihar is an excellent example. Personalities rather than principles play a dominant role. The parting with the JD(U) seems to have been due to interpersonal attitudes and caste pulls rather than ideology.

The Congress party did not pause to take a well-deserved rest after the strenuous and gruelling campaign. Soon after the results, the party announced fact-finding committees for Madhya Pradesh, Chhattisgarh, Odisha, Karnataka, Telangana, Delhi, Uttarakhand

---

[94]Tiwary, Deeptiman, and Nikhila Henry, 'Day after Meghwal says UCC still on table, ally JD(U) says only through consensus', *The Indian Express*, 13 June 2024, https://tinyurl.com/3s5xet4c. Accessed on 15 January 2025.

[95]'Most BJP allies refrain from supporting UCC, positive to simultaneous polls', *Business Standard*, 16 August 2024, https://tinyurl.com/4bwbu27h. Accessed on 15 January 2025.

and Himachal Pradesh. We may have to plan solely for contests where the glue of alliance has come unstuck—as in the case of the AAP in Delhi—or was never very firm in the first place. But the commitment to the INDIA Alliance is firm and transparent.

In the CWC meeting to review the election results, Rahul was unanimously requested to lead the party in the Lok Sabha. But he merely replied that he would think about it. Further entreaties, including the Congress president's, did not move him. Fortunately, closed-door persuasion seemed to work over the next few days, and he donned the mantle.

Our party cadres experienced a sense of celebration that our LoP in the Lok Sabha would make his presence felt as the leader on the Opposition benches, as indeed on the several important appointment committees. Clearly, the PM now has a match in the LoP and will need to watch his step. After all, the doubts the BJP propaganda machine created have been resolutely repudiated by the voters.

EPILOGUE

NEW POLITICS ON THE HORIZON

Many observers believe that the 2024 general election was an election of the people, by the people, for the people. In keeping with this spirit of democracy, Rahul Gandhi invited requests for all kinds of interviews and interactions. In a post on X, he said, 'Unhindered, unfiltered, undaunted—a free and fair conversation is the strength of our democracy! I am here to speak with you, listen to you, and facilitate the true expression of the idea of India.'[1] This starkly contrasts the carefully scripted interviews PM Modi gave in the run-up to and during the campaign. This, too, was a departure from the past when he gave interviews to a chosen few and carefully avoided press conferences. The latter trend continued, but he gave interviews galore, primarily to media persons who seemed to be in awe of the man—no Karan Thapars.[2,3,4]

Surprisingly, there has been little articulation about the election outcome from the BJP or its supreme leader, except to chant the defeat of the anti-incumbency to get a third term.

However, on the streets, there were signs that a wounded tiger was on the prowl. Suddenly, lynching incidents were reported in Assam, Bihar and Uttar Pradesh despite the provisions of the new criminal law. In all these incidents, the victims were Muslims. Two of these mob attacks resulted in the death of two men. Seemingly,

---

[1] @RahulGandhi, *X* (formerly Twitter), 2 July 2024, 1:52 p.m., https://tinyurl.com/58hpjfhj. Accessed on 15 January 2025.
[2] 'Modi versus media: Rajdeep on new crop of anchors, why some may be wearing "Bajrang Dal shorts"', *Newslaundry*, 23 December 2024, https://tinyurl.com/4nccpjna. Accessed on 15 January 2025.
[3] Deb, Abhik, 'Listening to 41 Modi interviews: Few tough questions, no rebuttals, no fact checks', *Scroll.in*, 19 May 2024, https://tinyurl.com/bdezb8kz. Accessed on 15 January 2025.
[4] Philiopose, Pamela, 'Backstory: Modi's Interviews Have Become More Artful (and More Plentiful) This Election Season', *The Wire*, 25 May 2024, https://tinyurl.com/yc6nh747. Accessed on 15 January 2025.

bovine protesters and 'cow vigilante squads' were running rampant across India, indulging in lynchings as a form of 'justice'.[5]

Such lynching is not a random act of violence committed against a soft target. It has a backdrop of enforcing the victim's perceived inferiority and vulnerability.[6][7] The violence inflicted is horrible in itself, but the intent to inflict indignity undermines civil society and constitutional values. These are experiments of destruction of everything India stands for and the basis of our contest between hate and compassion.

Sadly, confrontation, if not open conflict, seems to be the flavour of the outcome of the 2024 elections, as witnessed by raucous protests from both sides of the aisle in Parliament. In the Rajya Sabha, Chairman Jagdeep Dhankhar touched a sensitive chord in the heart of the grand warrior for social justice, Mallikarjun Kharge, Rajya Sabha LoP. The Chairman said Jairam Ramesh interrupted him during the proceedings and sarcastically referred to him as 'intelligent and talented' and ironically asked him to take over Kharge's position in Parliament.[8] A war of words was inevitable. The Chairman insisted that he had said this to preserve the LoP's dignity, while the latter complained of Varna fixation.

Whatever the leaders on either side might say, at best incremental gains have been made, although the outcomes remain inconclusive. While the invincibility of the Modi posture has been visibly dented, the Opposition is still struggling to impact the

---

[5]Ibid.
[6]Persyn, Kristin, 'Understanding Lynching: A Deep Dive into Its History and Impact', *iKno*, 10 December 2025, https://tinyurl.com/534xvrp3. Accessed on 15 January 2025.
[7]Shukla, Abhya, 'Lynchings in India: A doctor explains the pathology of normalising extreme violence', *Scroll.in*, https://tinyurl.com/3yxd9bbc. Accessed on 15 January 2025.
[8]'War of words between Dhankhar and Kharge in Rajya Sabha', *The Hindu*, 2 July 2024, https://tinyurl.com/4e4wx2ey. Accessed on 3 December 2024.

decision-making process; the government continues to mouth acronyms, claiming success in its failure, while the Opposition consistently underscores the need for substantive social justice.

In 2024, politics remain caught between symbolism, both fake and real, on the one hand, and a cry for justice on the other. The road ahead is challenging, but then we are led by a leader who traversed over 3,000 kilometres to carry the message of love to every home and heart. New politics is on the horizon.

'Unhindered, unfiltered, undaunted'

This new brand of politics, as well as the role and responsibilities of the LoP, which Rahul Gandhi ultimately accepted, played out admirably in his debut speech in the eighteenth Lok Sabha during the motion of thanks to the President's address. Without mincing words, he took on the BJP and even the Speaker, reminding him of the parliamentary protocol that made him above all, including the PM. 'Speaker sir, please forgive me for saying this [...] You are the final arbiter of what happens in the Lok Sabha [...] But I noticed something. When I shook your hand, you stood straight and shook your hand like this. When Modi ji shook your hand, you bowed down and shook your hand,' Rahul said, pointing out to the Speaker.[9] His questioning of the Hindu credentials of people who believed in hate and violence as a credo floored the ruling party, whose leader could say little more than accuse the LoP of being *balak buddhi* (childish intelligence).[10] Besides the unfairness

---

[9]Mahaprashasta, Ajoy Ashirwad, 'In Maiden Speech as LoP, Rahul Gandhi Tears into Modi Govt on Hate Politics, Price Rise and NEET', *The Wire*, 1 July 2024, https://tinyurl.com/2sv6jfra. Accessed on 3 December 2024.
[10]Pathak, Vikas, 'PM Modi on Rahul: Balak buddhi, insults Hinduism; LoP's remarks expunged', *The Indian Express*, 3 July 2024, https://tinyurl.com/2vhrezht. Accessed on 3 December 2024.

of his smacks towards the Opposition, it is horrendously incorrect if we go by our civilizational concern and respect for children and the celebration of Ram Lalla.

Rahul took the proverbial bull by the horns when he said, '*Daro Mat, Darao Mat* (Don't fear, don't scare others). This is the central message of all religions, including Lord Shiva.'[11] He concluded his speech by urging the government to collaborate without resorting to hostility towards the Opposition, emphasizing the need to work peacefully and without animosity.

Rahul's call for unity and non-aggression towards the Opposition reflects his commitment to non-violence and peaceful cooperation in political discourse. He emphasized the importance of working together without resorting to hostility or hatred, promoting a harmonious approach to governance and social change. This sentiment aligns with his philosophy of Satyagraha, which advocates non-violent resistance and constructive dialogue to achieve justice and progress. The rapid-fire questions during the two-hour speech left their mark. What followed was a litany of remarks being expunged from the record of the House.

Rahul touched a raw nerve but also flagged the need to understand Hinduism and liberty in the best sense. This is all at the popular level rather than the theological plane, informing popular debates to some extent. The time has come to end the ambiguity of Islamic formulations and precepts. Demonizing Islam or vilification of Hinduism are equally Nehru's formulations: 'It must be remembered that the communalism of a majority community must of necessity bear a closer resemblance to nationalism than the communalism of a minority group. One of the best tests of its true nature is the relation it bears to the national struggle. If

---

[11]Mahaprashasta, Ajoy Ashirwad, 'In Maiden Speech as LoP, Rahul Gandhi Tears into Modi Govt on Hate Politics, Price Rise and NEET', *The Wire*, 1 July 2024, https://https://tinyurl.com/2sv6jfra. Accessed on 3 December 2024.

it is politically reactionary or stresses communal problems rather than national ones, then it is obviously anti-national.' Decades later, his worthy great-grandson is at pains to show India and the world how to keep communalism and nationalism apart.[12]

The terms of engagement are clear and have been unambiguously stated not only by the LoP in the Lok Sabha but also by the former Congress president and leader of the Congress legislative party in her article in *The Hindu*.[13]

> *I would like to remind readers of what the INDIA bloc parties conveyed to the Prime Minister when his emissaries sought unanimity for the post of Speaker. Our response was simple and straightforward: we stated that we would support the government. However, in keeping with convention and tradition, it was only fair and reasonable to expect that the post of Deputy Speaker be allocated to a member from the Opposition. This perfectly reasonable request was deemed unacceptable by a regime that, it is worth recalling, failed to fill the Constitutional position of Deputy Speaker during the entire tenure of the seventeenth Lok Sabha.*
>
> *Subsequently, the Prime Minister and his party dredged up the Emergency—astonishingly, even the Speaker invoked it despite holding a position that demands strict impartiality and an absence of any public political stance. This attempt to divert attention from the assault on the Constitution, its foundational principles and values, and the institutions it establishes and empowers, casts a shadow over the prospects for the smooth functioning of Parliament.*

---

[12] Mukherjee, Mridula, 'Nehru's Word: On Hindu and Muslim communalism', *National Herald*, 2 January 2022, https://tinyurl.com/5n7rn8r5. Accessed on 3 December 2024.
[13] Gandhi, Sonia, 'Preaching consensus, provoking confrontation', *The Hindu*, 29 June 2024, https://tinyurl.com/4pf67zw5. Accessed on 3 December 2024.

> [...] The INDIA bloc parties have made it clear that they do not seek a confrontationist attitude. The Leader of the Opposition, Rahul Gandhi, has offered cooperation. The leaders of the constituents of the alliance have made clear that they are looking to being productive in Parliament and to impartiality in the conduct of its proceedings. It is our hope that the Prime Minister and his government will respond positively. The initial evidence does not augur well, but we in the Opposition are committed to restoring balance and productivity in Parliament, to ensure that the voice of the millions who have sent us there as their representatives is heard and their concerns are raised and addressed. We live in the hope that the Treasury benches will step forward so that we can fulfil our democratic duties.

So far, the government has shown little accommodation, though it is supposed to be commonplace in a parliamentary democracy. Yet, there is a sense of relief among common people and further hope prodded by the statements of leaders like Sharad Pawar and Lalu Prasad Yadav. Rahul raised the bar during his visit to Gujarat in July.[14]

Beyond the party workers in Ahmedabad and other parts of the country, Rahul's outreach is echoed by progressive and liberal political parties across the world in the connections nurtured by the Samruddha Bharat Foundation. Important speaking events at top universities have drawn hordes of young Indians looking to his leadership for a free society. The efforts of our right-wing rivals to infiltrate top universities and indoctrinate unsuspecting youth have found their match in the inspirational aura that Rahul exudes.[15]

---

[14] 'Rahul reiterates his call to defeat BJP in Gujarat', *The Hindu*, 6 July 2024, https://tinyurl.com/ycxbt57s. Accessed on 3 December 2024.

[15] Datta, Rajat, 'Depoliticisation of students is a cover for right-wing forces to take over universities', *Hindustan Times*, 17 March 2017, https://tinyurl.com/bdd2kryw. Accessed on 15 January 2025.

Even as Rahul's overseas trips are carefully planned by Sam Pitroda and the Congress units in different parts of the world to reach out to the Indian diaspora (now firmly entrenched in countries across the world), critical meetings with world leaders continue to take place. Soon after Rahul took over as LoP, election results from the United Kingdom saw a landslide victory for the Keir Starmer-led Labour Party. Rahul sent messages to the new prime minister and the outgoing prime minister, Rishi Sunak. Both the British Prime Minister and the Deputy prime minister, Angela Rayner, as well as the foreign secretary, David Lammy, have had useful discussions with Rahul, including during the latter's recent visits to the United Kingdom. The Congress party made special efforts to attend the 2023 Labour Party Conference and has maintained contact with its leadership. The incumbent Labour government will, of course, have to deal with the Modi government, but it will inevitably consult with the Opposition.

The fact that Rahul has assiduously reached out to top world leaders and developed relations with grace will work wonders for India in due course. India has had to carefully balance its position vis-à-vis the Ukraine-Russia war as well as the Israel-Palestine conflict. The Congress has expressed understanding of India's compulsions in our relations with Russia but hoped that while preserving those relations, we could do more to persuade Russia to accept a peaceful solution. That sadly has not been evident, even as Ukraine seems to have given up its hope of equitable positioning by India.

The devastation in Gaza continues unabated despite world opinion turning against Israel. But India is nowhere to be seen.[16] [17] Now, even the US envoy has sounded a caution against strategic autonomy in times of conflict. Our foreign policy seems to be moving from one isolated position to another, heading for a *cul-de-sac*.

Which Way Our Future Lies

Back home, PM Modi's fixation with 'one nation, one election' led to the setting up of a high-powered committee to look into the idea. On 14 March 2024, former president Ram Nath Kovind submitted the committee's 18,000-page final report to President Droupadi Murmu.[18] Among many things, the report suggested the following:

- Setting up an 'Appointed Date' after the general elections to mark the new electoral cycle from 2029. This will require extending the term of those state legislative assemblies that are due to expire before this date and prematurely dissolve others whose five-year term extends beyond this date.
- A total of 18 amendments to the Constitution, most importantly Article 83 (concerning the duration of the Houses of the Parliament) and Article 172 (concerning the duration of the state legislative assemblies), are required.
- States are required to ratify amendments to Article 324A (to allow simultaneous elections in panchayats

---

[16]Hasan, Zoya, 'Israel's brutality in Gaza, India's pin-drop silence', *The Hindu*, 15 October 2024, https://tinyurl.com/avptddxs. Accessed on 15 January 2025.
[17]'Lost voice: On India's abstention on the Gaza vote at the UN', *The Hindu*, 31 October 2023, https://tinyurl.com/5e6v9v3s. Accessed on 15 January 2025.
[18]Phukan, Sandeep, 'Ram Nath Kovind panel for simultaneous Lok Sabha, Assembly polls', *The Hindu*, 15 March 2024, https://tinyurl.com/3ez3ezx6. Accessed on 3 December 2024.

and municipal bodies) and Article 325 (to empower the ECI to create a common electoral roll and voter IDs with the help of the state election commissions) passed by the Parliament.[19]

The report of the high-level committee on simultaneous elections continued to lie on the shelf, but meanwhile, it was elections as usual. The parties began preparing for the next round of state assembly elections in Haryana, Jammu and Kashmir, Maharashtra and Jharkhand, which were barely months away. These elections were expected to be an indication of how these states would read parliamentary election results. We have long believed that the voter approaches parliament and assembly elections differently. The next round of state assembly elections was expected to test this proposition, except that the outcome of 2024 was not so clear that one could predict a different outcome. But the jury was out on which direction our future would go, given that the 2024 verdict was short of being decisive on endorsing the status quo of a decade or a mandate for change.

The results in Haryana soon reversed the conclusions drawn from the outcome of 2024—supposedly a sign of the future. Here, for the second time in succession, the electorate firmly rejected the Congress's victory—foretold months ahead of the polls based on consistent reports from the ground of a swell in the fortunes of the Congress and growing resentment against the incumbent government. The reasons for snatching defeat from the jaws of victory were not hard to find. The incumbent BJP government, which needed a change in leadership to stand a fighting chance, capitalized on the Jat-versus-others dynamic to rally the strength of 36 communities. Bhupinder Hooda, the state's tallest leader,

---

[19]High Level Committee Report on Simultaneous Elections in India 2024, https://tinyurl.com/3hn8dsu9. Accessed on 9 December 2024.

failed to leverage his stature. Internal party rivalries cost Congress dearly, depriving it of the chance to build on its performance in 2024. However, the jury is still out on how the EVMs brought out for counting showed a 99 per cent charge despite being used for voting and stored for several days afterward.[20] The BJP can take credit for maintaining on-par vote percentage with the Congress despite a 10-year anti-incumbency period.

Jammu and Kashmir, on the other hand, has much more to talk about despite our modest seat contribution. The fact that the demographic divide was sought to be accentuated by our adversaries was resolutely blocked by the Congress-Jammu and Kashmir National Conference (NC) coalition. For several years, the BJP devised plans to prevent the return of regional parties in Jammu and Kashmir, as well as keep the Congress sidelined. It seemed a touch-and-go situation when we sat down to work out the alliance with the NC following Kharge and Rahul's dramatic trip to Srinagar. Clearly, the forces inimical to us were determined to frustrate the negotiations and work on innumerable independents to muddy the valley. Ghulam Nabi Azad had quickly retreated from a bid to play the kingmaker, if not a contrived king, but many imponderables like Engineer Rashid were given a run of the battleground.

The Congress leaders had a tough choice given the general sentiment of support for the politics of Rahul Gandhi and the NC being sensitive to the threat of losing their dominance in the valley. When the General Secretary (Organization), K.C. Venugopal, and I arrived in Srinagar and visited Farooq Abdullah, he seemed recalcitrant and aggrieved. At one point, he even suggested that we have a cup of tea and tell the waiting media persons that it

---

[20] Nath, Damini, 'Why some Haryana EVMs showed 99% charge after Assembly polls counting', *The Indian Express*, 1 November 2024, https://tinyurl.com/3actrzrn. Accessed on 15 January 2025.

was all over. I pulled out reserves of my goodwill and simply refused to take no for an answer. 'What do you suggest?' The former chief minister asked. 'Let us accept friendly contests where we are unable to agree,' I responded. When he returned to the room after a brief break, the stalemate had finally been broken with the formula of friendly fights in six crucial seats.

We might have conceded extra space to our coalition partner, but it ensured that Jammu and Kashmir would come out of BJP's grip. The principle and practical politics issue, which we have put on the back burner for a greater cause, remains in many parts of India, where we have made seat adjustments. But that is a topic for another day. Meanwhile, the road ahead in Jammu and Kashmir is not easy, but at least a fresh beginning can be made. After ten years, electoral democracy has returned to the erstwhile state in form. The new government must work quickly to infuse substance into it. Undoubtedly, great statesmanship will have to be shown. Of course, it remains to be seen how the enemies of peace will react to destabilize the opportunities that have presented themselves.

Shaking off the dust of Haryana, we waited with bated breath for the elections in Maharashtra and Jharkhand, which the ECI strategically delayed for some inexplicable reasons. These two states, too, were expected to be poised for Congress victories based on the general election results. Jharkhand held its ground and maintained its tribal support despite a feverish and divisive BJP campaign spearheaded by Assam Chief Minister Himanta Biswa Sarma. However, Maharashtra came as a disappointment for the Congress and a lifeline for the BJP-led NDA.

In the lead-up to the elections, one could sense considerable self-assurance among the partners of Maha Vikas Aghadi (MVA), even as the ruling coalition (Mahayuti) appeared uncertain. To their credit, post the Parliament debacle, the BJP/NDA pulled out all stops and caught the Congress-Sharad Pawar-Uddhav Thackeray combine on the wrong foot, particularly with the Ladki Bahin yojana. Many quarters have raised serious questions about the conduct of the Maharashtra elections, including concerns over EVMs and VVPATs.

On the first day of the special three-day session of the Maharashtra Assembly for the oath-taking of the newly elected MLAs, the Opposition MVA MLAs decided not to take oath to protest against the alleged misuse of EVMs and the state government's refusal to conduct mock polls using ballot papers in Markatwadi, a village in the Malshiras assembly constituency.[21] This may not be the last of the protests, as reports from across Maharashtra indicate widespread public disillusionment—perhaps the most significant since doubts about the EVMs first surfaced years ago. Meanwhile, fissures have appeared within the India Alliance, with the Samajwadi Party withdrawing from the MVA over Babri Masjid-related comments by a Shiv Sena (UBT) leader. Furthermore, remarks by Samajwadi Party and TMC leaders regarding the leadership of the INDIA Alliance underscore that electoral defeat often unravels alliances built on ambition.

Yet, I believe that ultimately the onus rests on PM Modi to begin a fresh chapter in contemporary history. The face he presents to the world must also be seen at home. Society is in considerable trauma—the collapsing bridges of Bihar,[22] the recurring horror

---

[21]Bhalekar, Ritvick Arun, 'Maharashtra Assembly session erupts in protest over EVM tampering charges', *India Today*, 8 December 2024, https://tinyurl.com/39wss5nz. Accessed on 9 December 2024.
[22]'A brief history of Bihar bridge collapses', *Financial Express*, 10 July 2024, https://tinyurl.com/cmuadb93. Accessed on 15 January 2025.

of lynching in Aligarh,[23] the stampede in Hathras,[24] the repeated terrorist attacks in Jammu and Kashmir,[25] the Naxalite encounters in Madhya Pradesh,[26] the bulldozing of law offenders' homes,[27] etc. The answer to all this is dialogue, dialogue and dialogue. Democracy must have a place for dialogue and dissent. The pursuit of a liberal society raises the right to disagree to the highest level, but with a caution that such a right does not include the right to be disagreeable. Sadly, under the incumbent government, being disagreeable has overwhelmed the right to disagree.

---

[23] Pandey, Sanjay, 'Tension in UP's Aligarh after Muslim youth lynched to death over suspicion of theft', *Deccan Herald*, 19 June 2024, https://tinyurl.com/yyxt7m4r. Accessed on 15 January 2025.

[24] Shamim, Sarah, 'What caused the deadly stampede in Hathras, India?', *Al Jazeera*, 3 July 2024, https://tinyurl.com/yeveswv4. Accessed on 15 January 2025.

[25] 'JKNC holds BJP regime accountable; Rajnath Singh says "Not an issue of security lapses"', *The Times of India*, 2 November 2024, https://tinyurl.com/bdemzv44. Accessed on 15 January 2025.

[26] 'Madhya Pradesh Encounter: Naxalite Carrying Rs 14 Lakh Reward Shot Dead in Balaghat', *ETV Bharat*, 8 July 2024, https://tinyurl.com/mrjcsez3. Accessed on 15 January 2025.

[27] Malpani, Mehul, 'Fast-tracked bulldozer justice in Madhya Pradesh', *The Hindu*, 1 March 2024, https://tinyurl.com/3jna6wus. Accessed on 15 January 2025.

POSTSCRIPT

ALLIANCE POLITICS ON THE BRINK: NAVIGATING THE EXISTENTIAL CRISIS

As the Delhi elections unfolded, it became clear that unity and strategic planning within the Congress were crucial in shaping the Opposition's strength. Devender Yadav, Delhi Pradesh Congress Committee (DPCC) president, and Ajay Maken, MP Rajya Sabha and National Treasurer of the party, played a key role in ensuring the party remained focused on its core issues while navigating the challenges of the political landscape. Yadav's extensive yatra across Delhi helped reconnect the Congress with its traditional voter base, bringing attention to local grievances and reinforcing the party's commitment to social justice and grassroots engagement.

Our focus remained on highlighting the development achieved under the leadership of Sheila Dikshit, Delhi's longest-serving and most successful chief minister, who transformed Delhi into a modern and inclusive city. Her tenure was marked by infrastructure expansion, improved public transport and better urban governance, setting a benchmark for progress. The decision to field her son Sandeep Dikshit from New Delhi against former chief minister Arvind Kejriwal was part of that statement.

In contrast, the mismanagement of the state by the BJP central government and Kejriwal's administration became increasingly evident. The frequent power struggles between the Centre and the Delhi government only worsened the situation, leaving essential services in neglect and slowing down progress. Instead of collaborative governance, Delhi witnessed constant political confrontations that hindered effective administration.

The Congress went into the elections caught in a cleft stick of needing to displace the AAP to claw back its lost ground in the state, yet conscious that beginning to do that could initially help the BJP. The AAP had repudiated an alliance in Delhi long before any discussions could happen. Of course, the Delhi Congress workers were most disinclined to join hands with Kejriwal.

Not Just Electoral but Symbolic

The results of the Delhi elections were not unexpected. Many had anticipated the downfall of the AAP and when it happened, there was a sense of vindication among those who had long had reservations about Kejriwal's politics. His defeat was not just the defeat of a party, but the downfall of a man who had once positioned himself as the torchbearer of a new kind of politics—free of corruption, flamboyance and deceit.

Kejriwal had risen from the movement against corruption, rallying behind the cause that had captured the imagination of an entire nation. He had promised to cleanse the system, to be different, and to redefine governance. But over time, his image was dented, his credibility eroded, and the very people who had once championed his rise now found solace in his political setback.

In certain circles, there was an unmistakable sense of satisfaction over the AAP's loss. Many who had endured Kejriwal's sharp-tongued accusations, his often-exaggerated claims and his constant attacks on opponents, found poetic justice in his defeat. His relentless attacks on the Congress were particularly harsh, even though it was the Congress government's policies that had laid the foundation for many of the initiatives for which he took credit.

Yet, many who disagreed with the euphoria over his downfall chose to remain silent. They knew that Kejriwal had a knack for turning criticism into an attack on himself, portraying himself as a victim of political vendettas. His supporters, fuelled by a sense of false ideological purity, would never acknowledge his faults and instead lash out at anyone who dared to criticize him.

One of the most interesting aspects of this election was the Congress party's influence in 13 crucial seats—which the AAP lost by exactly the same margin that the Congress candidates had secured. This was not mere coincidence; it was a reflection of the Congress's continued presence in Delhi politics, despite its diminished strength.

The AAP supporters, however, refused to see reality. Instead of acknowledging their miscalculations, they blamed the Congress, accusing it of conspiring with the BJP to ensure the AAP's defeat. The irony of this accusation was not lost on those who had observed the political landscape closely. For years, Kejriwal had positioned himself as the primary opponent of both the Congress and the BJP, often equating the two as part of the same corrupt establishment. Now, when his party suffered a setback, his supporters found it convenient to shift the blame elsewhere rather than introspect on their own mistakes.

In all fairness to the Congress, there was never an intention of letting the BJP win. The goal was clear: to ensure that the AAP was humbled, that its arrogance was checked, and that Kejriwal and his party understood that they could not take the electorate for granted. However, the strategy was not to achieve this at the cost of a BJP victory. Unfortunately, the electoral dynamics played out in a way that benefited the BJP more than expected. Had there been a pre-poll alliance between the Congress and the AAP, the results could have been very different. Delhi could have been saved from the BJP's grip. But this alliance never materialized. Even though the Congress extended an olive branch to the AAP in various states, the response was never the same. Rahul Gandhi had even tried to forge an alliance in Haryana, but political compulsions prevented it from materializing. The Congress was always open to cooperation but never received the same treatment in return.

A Lesson in Political Realities

One of the biggest reasons for our defeat was the confusion among Muslim voters. Historically, Muslims in Delhi had been a reliable support base for the Congress. But this time, they found themselves caught between the AAP and the Congress, uncertain about which party to back. Despite Kejriwal's complete silence on the issues that mattered to them—CAA, NRC and the Delhi riots—many still chose to vote for the AAP, believing it was the stronger alternative to the BJP. This was a strategic miscalculation as their divided support only weakened the broader Opposition. Had there been a clear direction and a consolidated strategy, the anti-BJP vote could have been more effective. But in the absence of unity, confusion reigned and the results reflected this uncertainty.

One of the most interesting moves in this election was the decision to field Sandeep Dikshit against Kejriwal. Sandeep carried with him a legacy that was both powerful and nostalgic. His entry into the contest was seen as a smart move, a direct challenge to Kejriwal's claim of being the architect of Delhi's transformation. Sandeep represented the Congress's golden era in Delhi, a time when governance was about development and not theatrics. However, despite his hard work and the goodwill he carried, he could not manage to turn this into votes. The political landscape had changed and while he had the credibility, the electorate was not ready to rally behind the Congress just yet.

Another significant factor in this election was the role of digital media. Digital ads played a major role in shaping public perception, especially among working class and office-going electorate. Reels, YouTube shorts and targeted online campaigns had a significant impact, keeping the public engaged and shaping their political opinions. The BJP, in particular, leveraged digital media with ruthless efficiency. Their messaging was sharp, their outreach well-planned, and their ability to influence the narrative through digital platforms was considerable. The AAP, despite its strong social media presence, struggled to counter this wave, particularly in the wake of the liquor scam that had severely damaged Kejriwal's image.

The liquor scam, in fact, was a turning point. It shattered Kejriwal's carefully curated image of an outsider in traditional politics. Overnight, he was no longer the clean, incorruptible leader he had claimed to be. His insistence on calling this election a referendum backfired spectacularly. The public, when given a choice, chose the BJP over him. It was a direct rejection of his politics, a clear message that his alternate style of governance was no longer as appealing as it once was.

Yet there was an irony in all this. Kejriwal had spent years accusing Congress leaders of corruption without a shred of evidence. He had built his entire movement on the idea that the Congress was the root of all corruption in India, while presenting himself as the lone warrior of honesty. But when the tables turned and he found himself at the receiving end of similar accusations, he cried foul. The very methods he had used to discredit others were now being used against him and he had no defence.

The Delhi elections were a lesson in political reality. They exposed the fragility of alliances, the power of digital narratives, and the consequences of misplaced arrogance. Kejriwal's defeat was not just electoral, it was symbolic. It marked the fall of a leader who once promised a revolution but had instead become a prisoner of his own contradictions. In the end, it was the people who had the final say.

These elections also showed that the formidable voter base among the upper castes that the BJP had nurtured for years remained loyal. The Lokniti-CSDS survey[1] conducted during the elections revealed how the party consolidated its hold among

---

[1] Kumar, Sanjay, and Dhruv Pandey, 'How BJP crafted Delhi landslide with a coalition of upper caste, OBC groups', *The Indian Express*, 10 February 2025, https://tinyurl.com/4du33u5r. Accessed on 10 March 2025.

Brahmins (66 per cent), Vaishyas (66 per cent), Punjabi Khatris (67 per cent), and Rajputs (60 per cent). Moreover, the party made significant inroads into the OBC vote bank, garnering 55 per cent of the votes in this segment, though its appeal among Gujjars and Yadavs remained weaker.

Meanwhile, the AAP, which had governed Delhi for the past decade, struggled to expand beyond its traditional support base. While it retained a strong hold among Valmikis (67 per cent), Jatavs (59 per cent), and Muslims (65 per cent), the party's dependence on these demographics limited its ability to counter the broader appeal of the BJP.[2]

The SP's PDA campaign—a focused attempt to consolidate backward castes, Dalits and minorities—gained traction in Uttar Pradesh and Bihar. Yet, its effectiveness in Delhi and other states remained dependent on the Congress's organizational strength and pan-India appeal.

Despite being weakened in several regions, the Congress continued to be the only party with a truly national presence and a broad-based voter outreach. The regional allies of the INDIA bloc—SP, RJD and others—realized that their campaigns could only succeed if they remained in alliance with the Congress, ensuring a cohesive front against the BJP.

However, the election itself was not free from controversy, as political parties raised concerns over the deletion of voter names—a pattern similar to the allegations made in Maharashtra, where Rahul Gandhi alleged that over 3.9 million new names were added to the voter lists before the local elections, a figure surpassing the total number of voters added in the preceding five years.[3] These unexpected additions have raised suspicions about potential

---

[2]Ibid.
[3]'39L voters added in 5 months, alleges Rahul Gandhi', *The Economic Times*, 7 February 2025, https://tinyurl.com/bnvrxnwu. Accessed on 3 March 2025.

manipulation of the electoral rolls. The lack of transparency and delayed responses from the ECI only intensified public scepticism.

Kejriwal lodged a complaint with the ECI, alleging that the BJP manipulated the electoral roll in the New Delhi assembly constituency by adding 13,000 voters and deleting 5,500 entries to influence the election.[4] The ECI, however, dismissed these allegations, asserting that the electoral roll process was transparent and involved multiple checks, including sharing draft rolls with political parties for feedback.

Clearly, what set this election apart was not just the BJP's sweeping victory, but also the shifting electoral strategies within the Opposition. The INDIA bloc, which had been conceptualized as a united front against the BJP, faced critical challenges in its attempt to remain cohesive. One of its strongest electoral advantages came from Rahul Gandhi's consistent focus on caste census and protection of constitutional values. His emphasis on social justice resonated with the marginalized groups, giving the INDIA bloc a much-needed ideological anchor. But the alliance itself was fragile, with internal divisions threatening its effectiveness.

Had the INDIA bloc established a structured approach to resolving electoral differences, such scenarios could have been handled more effectively. Rather than allowing differences to fester, the INDIA bloc parties should have focused on bringing both the Congress and the AAP together on a common platform rather than preferring one party, ensuring a strategic collaboration that prioritized the larger goal of defeating the BJP. The absence of timely intervention and coordination not only weakened the bloc's collective strength but also fuelled doubts about its ability to function as a cohesive political force.

---

[4] "'Where did 13,000 people come from': AAP urges EC to probe 'manipulated' electoral roll', *The Times of India*, 10 January 2025, https://tinyurl.com/8j8nfzdj. Accessed on 3 March 2025.

'Physician, Heal Thyself'

Compounding these issues are recent legislative changes affecting the autonomy of the ECI. The enactment of the Chief Election Commissioner and Other Election Commissioners (Appointment, Conditions of Service and Term of Office) Act, 2023, has restructured the appointment process for the CEC and other ECs. This Act establishes a Selection Committee comprising the PM, a Cabinet Minister and the LoP in the Lok Sabha. Notably, the Chief Justice of India (CJI), who was previously part of the selection process as per a Supreme Court directive issued in March 2023, has been excluded under the new law.

Critics argue that this revised selection process may compromise the independence of the ECI as it potentially increases executive influence over appointments. Additionally, the Act equates the salary and conditions of service of the CEC and ECs to those of the Cabinet Secretary, a shift from the previous parity with Supreme Court judges. This change has raised concerns about the potential erosion of the ECI's authority and autonomy.

These developments have prompted a broader discourse on the need to safeguard the impartiality and transparency of India's electoral system. Ensuring the independence of the ECI is paramount to maintaining public trust in the democratic process. But might it be correct to say, 'Physician, heal thyself.'

Unified Approach to Opposition Politics

The INDIA alliance was envisioned as a formidable opposition to the BJP, but its execution in the key states like Haryana, Maharashtra and Delhi exposed several strategic missteps. Internal negotiations, conflicting demands and inability to balance alliances with grassroots realities played a significant role in the outcome.

In Maharashtra, Akhilesh Yadav had asked for five seats, a demand that was denied. Instead, he was allotted two seats—ones that his party had previously won—while the remaining were left open for a 'friendly fight'. This decision, rather than fostering unity, created friction, as the alliance failed to present a united front. In Haryana, Akhilesh sought one seat, but due to local dynamics, it was given to Vinesh Phogat. Things could have been coordinated better and allies accommodated in a manner that maximized electoral gains.

The situation with the AAP was even more challenging. Their demands exceeded what could have been realistically accommodated without undermining the Congress's own organizational strength. Granting the AAP more seats would have risked alienating party workers and local leaders, whose support was crucial for the alliance's success. The AAP's reluctance to compromise was evident in their eventual vote share, which did not justify their claims for a larger share in seat distribution.

The political landscape is undoubtedly transforming, and voters are becoming more aware of the real issues affecting governance and democracy. However, for the INDIA alliance to be truly effective, it must learn from these mistakes—prioritizing unity, strategic planning and a more proactive approach to safeguarding the electoral process.

The by-elections in UP, particularly the Milkipur election, highlighted the shifting political undercurrents in the state. Milkipur, a reserved constituency with a significant Dalit and backward caste voter base, witnessed an intense contest, reflecting the broader struggle for dominance between the INDIA alliance and the BJP. The BJP, leveraging its organizational strength and welfare-driven narrative, managed to consolidate votes, while the Opposition struggled with coordination and local-level dissatisfaction. The seat-sharing disagreements within the INDIA alliance also played a role, as internal friction affected grassroots mobilization. Additionally, reports of electoral irregularities, including voter-list discrepancies and administrative biases, raised concerns about the fairness of the election process. The results underscored the need for a more cohesive strategy by the Opposition, ensuring that alliances are not just on paper but are effectively translated into ground-level coordination and outreach.

The SP must also come to terms with the reality that fighting elections alone will not yield the desired results. The Milkipur by-election and recent electoral trends have shown that fragmentation within the Opposition only benefits the BJP. While SP remains a strong regional force, its influence is not enough to counter the well-oiled election machinery of the ruling party. The INDIA alliance is essential not just for seat-sharing, but also for consolidating anti-BJP votes and presenting a united ideological front. The reluctance to fully integrate with the INDIA alliance weakens the broader Opposition and dilutes the impact of the regional parties. The SP must recognize that a partnership with the Congress is not just a political necessity but a long-term strategy to ensure a more formidable challenge to the BJP in upcoming elections.

In today's political landscape, unity among democratic forces is more important than ever. The growing centralization of power, the weakening of independent institutions, and increasing concerns over electoral integrity highlight the need to safeguard the Constitution and uphold democratic values. India's strength has always been its pluralism, diversity and commitment to justice, and it is essential to ensure that these principles continue to guide the nation's progress.

The Chief Minister of Jammu and Kashmir, Omar Abdullah, pointed out that if INDIA was meant to be more than just a parliamentary election arrangement, then the alliance partners must find ways to work together even in the state elections.[5] His call for a structured mechanism within the bloc to address seat-sharing disputes reflects the urgent need for a more unified approach to opposition politics.

To do so, INDIA bloc parties must rise above narrow self-interests and work towards a shared vision for the country. In a democracy, differences in ideology and perspective are natural, but when democratic institutions and constitutional safeguards face challenges, it becomes crucial to find common ground and focus on what truly matters. The BJP's strong electoral machinery and its ability to consolidate support across regions make it necessary for those who believe in constitutional values to collaborate and build a collective vision. This is not just about elections, but about ensuring that democratic institutions remain robust, freedoms are protected, and governance remains inclusive.

India has always thrived when different voices come together for a larger cause. Now is the time to move beyond individual differences and short-term gains and work towards a future that ensures justice, equality and opportunity for all. A democracy flourishes when its people stand together to protect its foundational values, and that responsibility lies with all of us.

The recent political landscape has underscored an important reality—fragmentation weakens the opposition. Rahul Gandhi's emphasis on caste representation and constitutional safeguards has resonated with many, offering the INDIA bloc a strong ideological foundation. However, sustaining this momentum requires a long-term commitment to collaboration and shared purpose. Opposition forces must focus on common democratic values rather than differences, ensuring that the fight is not just

---

[5] "'If INDIA bloc was only for parliamentary polls, better wind it up': Omar', *Hindustan Times*, 9 January 2025, https://tinyurl.com/yvpznw6j. Accessed on 4 March 2025.

about elections, but about protecting the very fabric of India's democracy. Only through collective effort and a shared vision can a more inclusive and representative political landscape be secured for the future.

INDEX

5 Nyays, 83
2024 Lok Sabha elections, 37, 45, 80, 129

Aam Aadmi Party (AAP), 52, 54, 115, 144, 147, 148, 158, 177, 178, 179, 180, 182, 183, 185
Aazad Samaj Party, 132
Abdullah, Farooq, 40, 113, 170
Abdullah, Omar, Chief Minister of Jammu and Kashmir, 40, 186
ABP News, 77
Adani, Gautam, 30
Adani Group, 30
Adi Shankaracharya, 40
Adityanath, Yogi, Chief Minister of Uttar Pradesh, 44, 117, 131, 134
Advani, L.K., Deputy Prime Minister of India, 42
Agarwal, Poonam, 27
Ahluwalia, Montek Singh, Indian economist, 22
Akali Dal, 114
Alam, Izhar, 137
Alam, Maria, 137, 138
Aligarh, 101, 173
Ali Khan, Mohammed, 120
Allahabad, 135, 139
Allavaru, Krishna, 83, 84
Alliance Committee, 136
All India Congress Committee (AICC), xiii, 37, 152
All India Majlis-e-Ittehadul Muslimeen (AIMIM), 41, 58, 100
Ambedkar, B.R., 38, 104, 108, 140
Amethi, 77, 78, 112, 135, 136
Amroha, 25, 137
Andhra Pradesh, 17, 65, 103, 122, 127
Anyay Kaal, 5, 6, 8, 10, 17, 24
Apna Dal, 57, 58
Article 370, 39, 51
Asom Gana Parishad (AGP), 115
Assam, 66, 110, 118, 151, 152, 161, 171
AstraZeneca, 8
Axis My India Polls, 126
Ayodhya, ix, 51, 97, 117, 139, 140
Azad, Chandrasekhar, 132
Azad, Ghulam Nabi, Chief Minister of Jammu and Kashmir, 170
Azmi, Abu Asim, 55

Babbar, Raj, 142
Babri Masjid, 109, 172
Bachchan, Amitabh, 135
Bahujan Samaj Party (BSP), 25, 56, 91, 115, 129, 130, 132, 137, 139
Bajrang Dal, 15, 161
Bal Singh, Hartosh, 29
Banerjee, Mamat, 52, 151
Bano, Bilkis, 18
Bansgaon, 119

Banswara, 98, 99, 100, 117, 142
Bhadohi, 136
Bharat Adivasi Party (BAP), 142
Bharat Jodo NYAY Yatra, 155
Bharat Jodo Yatra, 37, 38, 39, 40, 45, 64, 76
Bharat Rashtra Samiti (BRS), 41, 150
Bharatiya Janata Party (BJP), ix, x, xi, xii, 3, 4, 5, 6, 10, 11, 14, 16, 18, 20, 24, 25-27, 35, 38, 41-45, 51, 53-57, 59, 66, 70, 72-74, 78, 88, 90-93, 97, 102-105, 108, 109, 111-114, 116-118, 121, 122, 125, 126, 128-136, 139-150, 152-154, 156-158, 161, 163, 166, 169, 170, 171, 173, 177, 179-187
Bhaskar, Swara, 39
Bhatt, Pooja, 39
Bidhuri, Ramesh, 25
Bihar, 35, 52, 53, 54, 66, 100, 118, 127, 143, 157, 161, 172, 182
Bihari Vajpayee, Atal, Prime Minister of India, 42, 113
Biswa Sarma, Himanta, 118, 151, 171
Black Paper, 5, 6, 7
Bombay High Court, 16
Braj Mandal Jalabhishek Yatra, 15

C Voter, 126
Caste Census, 17, 86
Central Bureau of Investigation (CBI), 23, 26, 73, 110, 155
Centre for the Study of Developing Societies (CSDS), 9, 20, 76, 134, 141, 181
Chandigarh, 54, 66, 83, 148
Chandni Chowk, 144
Chandra Ulaka, Rama, 146
Chandrachud, D.Y., Chief Justice of India, 155
Chandrasekhar, Rajeev, 149
Chavan, Ashok, 55, 148
Chidambaram, P., Union Minister of Finance, 26, 64, 105

Chintan Shivir, 35, 64, 89
Choudhary, Mahesh, 125
Choudhry, Kiran, 142
Citizenship (Amendment) Act (CAA), 11, 13, 21, 51, 67, 157, 180
CNX, 126
Communist Party of India (CPI), 40, 51
Congress party, ix, x, xiii, 3, 5, 23, 28, 35, 36, 38, 65, 66, 68, 77, 79, 80, 81, 85, 86, 88, 89, 94, 110, 120, 121, 136, 139, 157, 167, 178
Congress Working Committee (CWC), 36, 45, 80, 89, 158
COVID-19, xi, 7, 8, 141
Covishield, 8
Criminal Procedure Code 1973, 23

Dalits, 17, 90, 92, 101, 104, 105, 129, 132, 133, 134, 182
Danish Ali, Kunwar, 25, 137
Delhi, 7, 11, 12, 13, 14, 19, 20, 21, 26, 30, 31, 42, 52, 54, 55, 65-67, 83, 84, 89, 143, 144, 148, 154, 155, 157, 158, 177-184
Delhi High Court, 7, 12
Delhi Police, 11, 12, 20, 31
Delhi Pradesh Congress Committee (DPCC), 177
Delhi School of Economics, 84
Delhi University, 67
democracy, x, xi, 24, 25, 47, 79, 80, 87, 106, 138, 161, 166, 171, 185, 187, 188
Deora, Milind, 148
Dhankhar, Jagdeep, 162
Dikshit, Sandeep, 144, 177, 180
Dikshit, Sheila, Chief Minister of Delhi, 177
Doval, Ajit, 12
Dravida Munnetra Kazhagam (DMK), 40, 52, 53
Dubey, Amitabh, 5, 69, 86
Dubey, Vikas, 135

Dwivedi, Harish, 140

Election Commission of India (ECI), x, 28, 51, 63, 75, 79, 117-122, 138, 151, 169, 171, 182, 183, 184
Electoral Bonds Scheme, 27, 28
Electronic voter machines (EVMs), 63, 119, 170, 172
Enforcement Directorate (ED), 23, 73
Extremely Backward Classes (EBCs), 130, 131, 133

Fadnavis, Devendra, 114
Faizabad, 140
Fatehpur Sikri, 119, 136, 137

G20 Summit, 21
Gadkari, Nitin, Minister of Road Transport and Highways, Government of India, 44
Gandhi, Indira, 5, 78, 107, 111, 112
Gandhi, Mahatma, xiv, 22, 40, 64
Gandhi, Maneka, Minister of Women and Child Development, Government of India, 114, 140
Gandhi, Rahul, Leader of the Opposition of Lok Sabha, ix, xiii, 6, 9, 25, 28, 36, 37, 39, 40, 76, 77, 89, 101, 102, 111, 112, 114, 125, 128, 129, 135, 155, 161, 163, 164, 166, 170, 179, 182, 183, 187
Gandhi Vadra, Priyanka, 19, 40, 78
Gandhi, Varun, 112, 114
Gaza, 167, 168
Gehlot, Ashok, Chief Minister of Rajasthan, 54, 68, 141
Godi media, 70
Godse, Nathuram, 46
Gopal Yadav, Ram, Secretary General of the Samajwadi Party, 55
Govil, Arun, 139
Goyal, Piyush, 114
Guha Thakurta, Paranjoy, 31

Gujarat, 18, 30, 44, 54, 65, 67, 103, 127, 166
Gujral, I.K., Prime Minister of India, 114
Gujral, Naresh, 114
Gurugram, 14, 15, 142

Hain Taiyaar Hum campaign, 65
Haryana, 15, 66, 92, 127, 142, 169, 170, 171, 179, 184, 185
Hathras, 10, 18, 31, 173
Hathras gangrape case, 31
Hindutva, 4, 38, 131, 135

Ilaiah, Kancha, 93
Income Tax Department, 28, 79
INDIA Alliance, 4, 35, 53, 56, 57, 59, 64, 97, 109, 118, 125, 128, 129, 132, 133, 134, 148, 151, 157, 158, 172
INDIA bloc, 53, 90, 91, 92, 108, 126, 133, 139, 165, 166, 182, 183, 187
India Today, 19, 76, 77, 78, 90, 92, 97, 117, 126, 129, 138, 147, 151, 172
Indian Muslims for Civil Rights, 110
Indian National Congress, 3, 36, 45, 71, 72, 80, 89, 103, 149
Indian Penal Code 1860, 23
Indian Premier League (IPL), 72
Indian Union Muslim League (IUML), 40, 149
International Olympic Committee (IOC), 20
Irani, Smriti, Minister of Education, 118, 135, 136
Israel, 167, 168

Jaffrabad, 11
Jain, Sreenivasan, 30
Jaiswal, Sriprakash, 136
Jalandhar, 147
Jamia Millia Islamia, 11, 67
Jammu and Kashmir, 37, 39, 40, 66, 113, 169, 170, 171, 173, 186
Jammu and Kashmir National

Conference (NC), 40, 170
Jan Ki Baat, 126
Jan Sangh, 42
Jantar Mantar, 20
Jawaharlal Nehru University, 67

Kannauj, 131, 133
Kanpur, 56, 136
Kanyakumari, 37, 40
Kappan, Siddique, 31
Kargil War, 137
Karnataka, 5, 16, 24, 41, 65, 66, 91, 92, 102, 104, 106, 127, 150, 157
Kavitha, K., 150
Kejriwal, Arvind, Chief Minister of Delhi, 26, 52, 77, 177, 178, 179, 180, 181, 182
Khabri, Brijlal, 136
Khalid, Umar, 13
Khan Market Gang, 14
Kharge, Mallikarjun, President of the Indian National Congress, 6, 38, 52, 69, 78, 79, 80, 89, 162, 170
Khurshid, Louise, 111
Kisan Nyay, 81, 82
Kishor, Prashant, 35, 143
Kovind, Ram Nath, President of India, 168
Kukis, 152, 153, 154
Kumar Bansal, Pawan, 148
Kumar, Kanhaiya, 144
Kumar, Nitish, Chief Minister of Bihar, 52
Kumar, Ravish, 30, 31, 70

Lakhimpur Kheri, 19
Lal, Devi, Deputy Prime Minister of India, 113, 114
Lal Sharma, Bhajan, 42
Lal Sharma, Kishori, 135
Lammy, David, 167
Lilothia, Rajesh, 93
Lingayat, 91, 92
Lokniti survey, 20

Lord Ram, 97, 139, 140

Madhya Pradesh, 24, 26, 41, 42, 43, 44, 65, 97, 127, 144, 157, 173
Maharashtra, xii, 18, 24, 26, 54, 55, 65, 91, 108, 112, 127, 148, 169, 171, 172, 182, 184, 185
Maken, Ajay, Treasurer, All India Congress Committee, 28, 69, 78, 177
Malik, Sakshi, 20, 21
Mandal, Nishant, 119
Mandela, Nelson, xiv
Manipur, 10, 24, 45, 46, 66, 152, 153, 154, 155
Masood, Imran, 136
Matondkar, Urmila, 38
Meerut, 139
Meghnad, 32
Meiteis, 152, 153, 154
Milkipur, 185, 186
Mishra, Ajay, Minister of State for Home Affairs, 19
Mishra, Kapil, 11
Mishra, Sohit, 32
Misra, Alok, 136
Misra, Saket, 140
Mistry, Madhusudan, 142
Model Code of Conduct, 25, 115, 121
Modi, Narendra, Prime Minister of India, ix, x, xi, xii, xiii, 3-6, 8-12, 14, 18, 20-23, 29-31, 43-45, 51, 58, 63, 69, 70, 73-78, 97-110, 117, 134, 136, 138, 142, 155, 157, 161-164, 167, 168, 172
Modinomics, 6
Moily, Veerappa M., Minister of Power, Government of India, 87
Moitra, Mahua, 25
Molotov cocktails, 12, 15
Mufti, Iltija, 40
Mufti, Mehbooba, Chief Minister of Jammu and Kashmir, 40, 114

Murmu, Droupadi, President of India, 168

Naari Nyay, 81, 85
Nadda, J.P., Minister of Chemicals and Fertilizers, Government of India, 44, 69
Nagina, 132
Nandan Bahuguna, Hemwati, 135
Narasimha Rao, P.V., Prime Minister of India, 114
Nath, Kamal, 26, 144
National Conference (NC), 40, 170
National War Room, 66, 67, 119
Nehru-Gandhi dynasty, 111
Nehru, Jawaharlal, Prime Minister of India, ix, 67, 89, 108, 111, 112
New Delhi Television (NDTV), 18, 19, 30, 63, 130, 138, 142
NewsClick, 31, 130
Nishad, Rambhual, 140
Northeast Delhi, 11, 144
Nuh, 15
NYAY Patra, 45

Owaisi, Asaduddin, 110, 150

Patel, Ahmed, 54
Pathan, Yusuf, 151
Patnaik, Naveen, Chief Minister of Odisha, 112, 146
Peace Party of India, 110
Pegasus, 28, 29
People's Democratic Party (PDP), 40
Pilot, Sachin, 114, 141
Pitroda, Sam, 105, 107, 167
Planning Commission, 22, 23
Poonam Agarwal, 27
Pran Pratishtha, ix
Prasad Chaudhary, Ram, 140
Prasad Singh, Akhilesh, 143
Prasad Yadav, Lalu, 113, 166
Prayagraj, 135
Punia, Bajrang, 20, 21

Punia, Vineet, 69
Purkayastha, Prabir, 31

Rae Bareli, 77, 78, 135, 136
Rai, Ajay, President of Uttar Pradesh Congress Committee, x, xii, 56, 58, 139
Rajan, Raghuram, Governor of the Reserve Bank of India, 39
Rajasthan, 41, 42, 65, 67, 68, 92, 97, 98, 112, 117, 125, 127, 135, 141, 142
Raje Scindia, Vijaya, 42
Raje, Vasundhara, Chief Minister of Rajasthan, 42, 112
Raju, K., 93
Ramayan, 139
Ramesh Bidhuri, 25
Ramesh, Jairam, 37, 53, 67, 70, 74, 86, 162
Ram Janmabhoomi, ix
Ram Rajya, 139
Ram Temple, ix, 3, 51, 97, 140, 141
Ram Van Gaman Path project, 140
Ranganath Misra Commission Reports, 104
Ranjan Chowdhury, Adhir, 151
Rao, K. Chandrasekhar, 150
Rashid, Engineer, 170
Rashtriya Swayamsevak Sangh (RSS), 3, 44, 46, 63
Razdan, Nidhi, 30
Reddy, Revanth, Chief Minister of Telangana, 150
Russia, 51, 167
Russia-Ukraine war, 51

Sachar Committee Report, 99
Saharanpur, 136
Samajwadi Party, xii, 55, 56, 57, 58, 59, 129, 131-134, 137, 139, 172
Samruddha Bharat Foundation (SBF), 88
Sanatana Dharma, ix, x
Sangma A., Saleng, 152

Santosh, Varun, 5, 37, 74
Scheduled Caste (SC), 10, 17, 82, 87-93, 98, 100, 103, 105, 108, 128, 132
Scheduled Tribes (ST), 10, 82, 89, 92, 93, 98, 100, 103, 105, 108, 128
Scroll, 22, 97, 98, 99, 100, 152, 161, 162
Selja, Kumari, 142
Sengar Singh, Kuldeep, 18
Sen, Riya, 39
Senthil, Sasikanth, 67, 120, 122
Setalvad, Teesta, 31
Shaffer, Peter, xiv
Shaheen Bagh, 11, 21
Sharan Singh, Bhushan, Brij, President, Wrestling Federation of India, 20, 21
Shastri, Lal Bahadur, Prime Minister of India, 114
Shastri, Sunil, 139
Shiv Sena, 26, 55, 113, 148, 172
Siddaramaiah, 41
Siddhapeeth Baba Gauri Shankar Mahadev, 131
Siddique, Baba, 148
Siddiqui, Nasimuddin, 136
Sikarwar, Ramnath Singh, 136
Singh, Amritpal, 147
Singh, Biren N., Chief Minister of Manipur, 153
Singh Channi, Charanjit, 147
Singh, Charan, Prime Minister of India, 113, 114
Singh Chautala, Ranjit, 114
Singh Chouhan, Shivraj, Minister of Agriculture and Farmers Welfare, Government of India, 42, 43, 113, 144
Singh, Digvijaya, 144
Singh Hooda, Bhupinder, 142
Singh Khalsa, Sarabjeet, 147
Singh, Lallu, 140
Singh, Manmohan, Prime Minister of India, 70, 99, 106

Singh, Rewati Raman, 135
Singh, Shubhkaran, 19
Singh, Ujjwal Raman, 135
Sitharaman, Nirmala, Minister of Corporate Affairs, Government of India, 5, 76
Soren, Hemant, Chief Minister of Jharkhand, 26
Srinagar, 39, 40, 170
State Bank of India (SBI), 28
Sukhu, Sukhvinder Singh, Chief Minister of Himachal Pradesh, 26, 146
Sunak, Rishi, Prime Minister of the United Kingdom, 167
Supreme Court, ix, 13, 16, 18, 25, 26, 27, 28, 31, 63, 73, 104, 135, 152, 184
Suvidha App, 121

Tamil Nadu, 54, 55, 65, 66, 91, 100, 127
Telangana, 41, 64, 65, 66, 110, 127, 149, 150, 157
Telugu Desam Party (TDP), 115, 126
Tewari, Manish, 148
Thackeray, Uddhav, Chief Minister of Maharashtra, 113, 148, 172
Thakur, Anurag, 11, 112, 114, 118
Tharoor, Shashi, 38, 149
The Caravan, 29, 42, 43
The Kashmir Files, 32
Thrissur, 149
Tilak Swaraj Fund, 64
Times Now, 98, 131
Today's Chanakya, 126
Trump, Donald, US President, 11, 21
Tukde Tukde Gang, 14
Tyagi, Devvrat Kumar, 139

Udaipur, 35, 36, 64, 89
Ukraine, 51, 167
Uniform Civil Code (UCC), 16, 51, 135, 157

United Progressive Alliance (UPA), 3, 8, 22, 70, 88
United World Wrestling (UWW), 20
University of Hyderabad, 17
Unlawful Activities (Prevention) Act (UAPA), 14, 31
Unnao, 18
Uttar Pradesh, x, xii, 35, 44, 55, 56, 66, 88, 91, 108, 112, 114, 118, 119, 127, 129, 130, 132, 133, 134, 141, 161, 182
Uttar Pradesh Congress Committee (UPCC), 56, 58, 136, 139

Varanasi, xii, 58, 59, 136, 138, 140
Vemula, Radhika, 39
Vemula, Rohith, 17
Venugopal, K.C., 69, 170
Vishva Hindu Parishad (VHP), 15
vote jihad, 137, 138

West Bengal, xii, 66, 122, 127, 151
World Press Freedom Index, 30
Wrestling Federation of India (WFI), 20, 21

Yadav, Akhilesh, Chief Minister of Uttar Pradesh, 52, 55, 112, 129, 131, 185
Yadav, Devender, 177
Yadav, Mulayam Singh, Minister of Defence, Government of India, 113, 133
Yadav, Pappu, 143
Yadav, Tejashwi, Deputy Chief Minister of Bihar, 52
Yadav, Yogendra, 37, 125
Youth Congress, 68, 83, 84
Yuva Nyay, 81, 84

Zargar, Safoora, 13